The lyrics haunted her....

How could I have stopped you.
But why did I let you go?
More than my soul died with you.
Life is a teacher,
And love is the lesson,
Belatedly, bitterly true...

Directed by the poignant regret in the song, Carla's eyes strayed to a dim white shape at the other end of the booth. Fletcher leaned one arm against the spotlight bay, his forehead pressed against it and his eyes forlorn. Did the song so affect him? Did he still think in misery of the girl who had died, the girl he'd shared so much with?

Carla felt a sudden, acute misery. What had *she* shared with him? She was nothing to him but a liability. She hadn't wanted to discover warm feelings for this man, but there they lay, as messy and unavoidable as a flooded basement.

She loved him.

Dear Reader,

Although our culture is always changing, the desire to love and be loved is a constant in every woman's heart. Silhouette Romances reflect that desire, sweeping you away with books that will make you laugh and cry, poignant stories that will move you time and time again.

This year we're featuring Romances with a playful twist. Remember those fun-loving heroines who always manage to get themselves into tricky predicaments? You'll enjoy reading about their escapades in Silhouette Romances by Brittany Young, Debbie Macomber, Annette Broadrick and Rita Rainville.

We're also publishing Romances by many of your all-time favorites such as Ginna Gray, Dixie Browning, Laurie Paige and Joan Hohl. Your overwhelming reaction to these authors has served as a touchstone for us, and we're pleased to bring you more books with Silhouette's distinctive medley of charm, wit and—above all—*romance*. I hope you enjoy this book, and the many stories to come.

Sincerely,

Rosalind Noonan
Senior Editor
SILHOUETTE BOOKS

LYNNETTE MORLAND
Camera Shy

Silhouette Romance

Published by Silhouette Books New York

America's Publisher of Contemporary Romance

To Celeste,
for her good taste and generosity

SILHOUETTE BOOKS
300 E. 42nd St., New York, N.Y. 10017

Copyright © 1985 by Karen O'Connell

Distributed by Pocket Books

ISBN: 0-373-08399-8

First Silhouette Books printing November 1985

10 9 8 7 6 5 4 3 2 1

America's Publisher of Contemporary Romance

Printed in the U.S.A.

Books by Lynnette Morland

Silhouette Romance

Occupational Hazard #339
Camera Shy #399

LYNNETTE MORLAND

lives in New York and considers it the most glorious city in the universe (although she plans to give London a chance to snatch the title). She loves antique clothing, drinking espresso in Greenwich Village cafés, reading in bed and staying up all night to write her books.

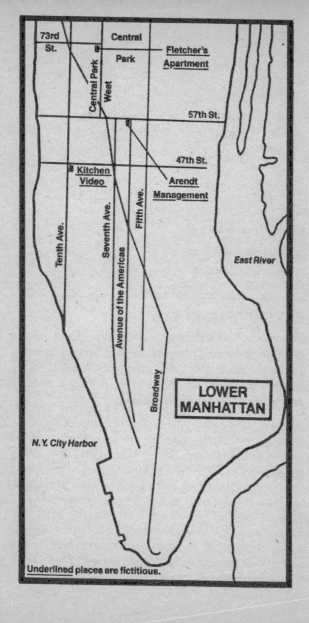

73rd
St.

Central

Park

Central Park West

Fletcher's
Apartment

57th St.

47th St.

Kitchen
Video

Arendt
Management

Tenth Ave.

Seventh Ave.

Avenue of the Americas

Fifth Ave.

East River

Broadway

LOWER
MANHATTAN

N. Y. City Harbor

Underlined places are fictitious.

Chapter One

Two bored and snobbish-looking bouncers lounged in front of the door to Weeds, keeping back a gaggle of teenage girls, each of whom was flushed with excitement and dressed to the outer limits of fashion. The sight annoyed Carla. She was very democratic—she hated the fact that whenever one found celebrities one found a door with a guard. Outside stood the fans, people who adored the celebrities, made them successful, and got treated like peons. Inside one found the privileged few who, often for no good reason, could saunter unchallenged into clubs like Weeds while everyone else had to sweat it out on the sidewalk.

She also hated to admit that this time she was one of the lucky ones who could saunter in. Not quite unchallenged, however. One guard, the one wearing an obscene T-shirt stretched over his beer belly, stopped her with a hairy arm.

"Sorry, sweetie, can't go in there."

Carla coldly held a sheet of Telemusic Cable TV stationery in front of his loutish face and hoped fervently that he had the mental capacity to read. His eyes struggled down the page, his face falling into an even uglier expression. Carla thought with grim satisfaction of the wording of the letter:

Hey Carla,

Where have you been hiding yourself these last two million years? Still in the filmmaking business (I hope)? If so, I have a BIG PROJECT TO DISCUSS WITH YOU!! My schedule is, as usual, *intense*—why don't you pop down to the Weeds next Tuesday afternoon? I'm interviewing the new rock god (Billy Pilgrim, in case you're out of touch with modern civilization) for Telemusic's *Fresh Faces* show and ought to have a few minutes free to explain my proposition to you afterward. Sorry everything's such a rush.

Dietra

P.S. Tell those Neanderthal bouncers at Weeds that if they don't let you in I'll have the club cut off their beer ration for a *month!* (There's a threat they'll take seriously.)

The T-shirted Neanderthal glanced at Carla. Carla glared back, wishing she looked more like a twenty-five-year-old independent filmmaker and less like a dizzy-headed kid—less like Dietra, in fact.

"What's your last name?"

"Copeland," she replied, tugging the letter from his stumpy fingers.

"I'll have to check the list," he insisted stubbornly.

Carla ground her teeth. It'd be just like Dietra to have forgotten to add her name to the door list.

"Humph," T-shirt grunted. "Go on. They're filming upstairs."

Before he could find a fresh way to detain her, Carla slipped inside. Weeds had once been a grand Art Deco ballroom, boasting wide, marble staircases and mirrored cloakrooms. It looked now as if it also had been used for artillery practice: the staircases were chipped and crooked, the velvet wallpaper torn off in long rags and splotched with posters and grafitti. The great gilt mirrors, fly-specked and murky, reflected this shabbiness over and over. Carla felt right at home; her studio looked much the same.

Even more uplifting was the sight that awaited her at the top of the stairs. The great dance floor twinkled under reflections from an enormous gilt chandelier. The stage was screened by heavily tasseled red curtains, and paper streamers from a recent party dripped over the balcony railings. Cameras, lights on tall tripods, umbrella-shaped reflectors and snaking cables clotted the worn parquet floor. Familiar noises reverberated through the soaring space—the sound check of a camera crew. "One, two. . .testing. . . Mike, can you give me a level on number four?. . .Thank you."

Carla's grim expression melted away. She loved film and the people who made it. As the daughter of a successful movie producer, Carla had grown up with two choices— adore the business or loathe it. She managed to do both. She loathed the glitzy side, the parties, the insincere flattery, the self-indulgence, but she had fallen hard for the craft and skill that built the industry. She could have ridden on her mother's reputation and gotten any kind of a job she wanted in movies. Instead she had struggled through four brutal years of film school and four even more brutal years, setting herself up as a serious, independent filmmaker. Things were not easy for her yet; Kitchen Video barely held its own from month to month, though projects were abundant, but she had the satisfaction of running her own show and knowing that every inch of progress had been gained through her own hard work.

Someday she'd be able to afford equipment as elaborate and professional as the Telemusic rig she saw before her in the ballroom. Until then she'd settle for coaxing advice from the Telemusic technicians. She headed for a friendly looking cameraman standing idle by a stack of Fresnel lights, but was intercepted by a skinny young man in pencil-thin black pants and a cutoff black sweat shirt. His dark hair was a mass of waves barely subdued by mousse. Despite his dangerously pointy-toed boots and his skull-and-crossbone earring, he had an appealing baby face.

"Dietra Sharpe?" he asked uncertainly.

"What? No," Carla replied kindly. All through film school she and Dietra had looked vaguely alike—same average height and lithe build, same wild, shoulder-length curls. But beneath the mop of hair Carla's face was small-featured and delicate (a fact that annoyed her to no end), Dietra's bolder and more strictly beautiful. Now that Carla's cable-TV celebrity friend had taken to dyeing her hair bright red, the resemblance was not so strong, but now and then people came up to Carla for Dietra Sharpe autographs.

The young man continued to stare, clearly perplexed.

"Sorry." Carla smiled. "Believe me, you'll know her when you see her. I'm just a lowly friend—Carla Copeland."

The boy recovered and shook her proffered hand. "Billy Pilgrim," he replied.

Ah, the rock god. He didn't look menacing enough, if she remembered his face from the posters. Cameras could lie so well.…"Look, Billy, don't worry if Dietra's not here yet—she always manages to turn up when the cameras are ready to roll.'' His hangdog expression engaged her sympathy. ''Hey, you know she wouldn't blow a chance to interview *you*.''

He smiled, wiggling a little, like a puppy who had been patted on the head. He seemed so young to be in a business this callous. Carla hoped he had someone trustworthy looking after him.

Without warning, they were descended upon by several shrieking girls who had somehow gotten past the guards. Billy grinned in delight and Carla faded gratefully into the shadows, only too happy to turn him over to his fans. Now where was that nice cameraman?

As she sought her quarry, she spied a commanding silhouette in the doorway near the stairs. A man had paused there, tall and menacing, with no detail clear but his lithe, powerful build. The professional in Carla itched to pick up a camera.

The man completed his survey of the ballroom and began to walk forward, passing from stark shadow into glittering light. Carla found herself watching him for reasons that no longer had to do with video—he was gorgeous. He looked about thirty-five and combined the solid dignity of a mature man with the swift energy of a young one. His camel-colored trousers sheathed long, clean-muscled legs and lean hips. Beneath his jacket a silk shirt of gold and olive checks showed off the broad, deep chest of a swimmer. Pale golden hair with streaks of white-blond flowed in careless waves around a tan, strong-featured face. But it was his ice-blue eyes that held Carla in a fascinated trance. Beneath dark brows that flared like hawk's wings, they shone with an electric power. They were slightly tipped, giving him an exotic look accentuated by his high, Tartar cheekbones and the tersely thinned line of his mouth. She knew stage presence when she saw it. Quite involuntarily, she backed up a step.

"That's it, ladies," he said in a low but penetrating voice. Every one of the girls looked around, their giggling suspended. "You'll have to see Billy on his tour—we're going to tape an interview now."

Carla would have thought nothing short of dynamite could blast the girls from their idol's side, but they fled like frightened children. She felt rather sorry for them. The blond man spared them barely a glance and turned to the deserted rock star with a smile that changed his whole countenance to one of warmth and encouragement. "You've got to stop being such a heartbreaker, Billy. You're downright cruel."

Billy grinned self-consciously, obviously pleased. "Yeah, but they left in a hurry when you told them to."

The blond man chuckled. "That's just because I'm so mean. That's what you pay me for." A casual turn revealed Carla to him. He frowned and left his young friend. "You, too, honey."

Too surprised to move, Carla stood frozen as he closed in on her. He didn't think she was a *fan,* did he?

"Sorry," he goaded and then, to her horror, he slapped her on the bottom. "Everyone out."

Without considering, she hit him. It was just an open-palmed slap, but she packed more punch than her delicate frame suggested. The blond man put his hand up to his reddening cheek and regarded her in amazement. In the background a low laugh was abruptly cut off.

Carla took hold of herself, appalled that she had lost her temper without a thought. "Would you care to rephrase that? Perhaps as an apology?" The silence around them vibrated with curiosity. Billy chewed furiously on a stick of gum, the technicians hid their eyes behind clipboards. But the blond let the seconds strain by, taking a long, interested look at Carla from her dingy sneakers to her untamable hair.

To her annoyance, his eyebrows lifted in an easy smile. To her astonishment, he said, "Yes, I will." The heads of cameramen rose and swiveled toward him. "That was a rather standard male chauvinist move on my part, wasn't it?"

"Quite standard," she agreed.

He frowned in mock concern. "Well, if you stay around, I'm bound to think up something quite original. Perhaps you'd like to leave first—*voluntarily.*"

"Sorry, I'm afraid I'm supposed to be here."

"I hope you're not going to tell me you're Dietra Sharpe's stunt double or something."

"No, but I *do* have business with her and she, in her inscrutable wisdom, suggested that I come here so we could discuss it after the taping."

"What kind of business?"

This was getting tedious. With any other man she would have spat out something terse and walked away, leaving him to his own interpretations. Somehow she felt it a bit dangerous to turn her back on this one. "*Video* business. My company is Kitchen Video." She said it as if he surely would have heard of it; she did not wish to specify that she *was* Kitchen Video, lock, stock and light meter.

To her unexpected rescue came one of the nearby soundmen. "Oh, yeah! Dietra said to expect you!"

Now you say that, Carla grumbled to herself, but the observation came soon enough to prevent another, more effective attack by this imperious man.

"All right," he conceded generously, implying that only his permission kept her from an extremely dire fate. A lazy grin curled the mobile mouth, revealing a dimple that would have been charming had he not already made such a bad impression on her. "I'll buy that. But," and his surprisingly dark-lashed eyes narrowed in warning, "if I come back and find you're still impersonating an underfoot fan, you're following the others out the door any way I can manage it." He turned easily on his heel and strode back into the gloom. As he passed Billy he said, "I'm going up to the office to work out a few things with Max. Yell if you need me. Oh, and I got the flowers for your mom's birthday."

Billy's face beamed with delight. "Thanks!"

"No problem, kid. Just remember to plug the album and the tour with Sharpe."

Carla felt a treacherous release of tension as his tall form vanished from the ballroom. It had taken all her mettle to keep from flinching under his assault. Not many people did that to her. Carla's own mother, a formidable personality in the industry, had lost battles with her.

With the blond man gone, the entire ballroom seemed to breathe easier. The technicians joked again and Billy, after looking woefully at the door that had cut him from view, drew himself up a little straighter, consciously adopting some of the other's confidence.

Dietra blew in on a breeze of chatter and cheerful buoyancy. "Hey, Jimmy! Reg! Hello up there, Leon! Tighten those bolts—you let one of those lights fall on my head and my hairdresser is out a fortune. Hi, Carla!" She dashed over and threw her arms around her friend. "You're as ragged as ever."

"Standard uniform for artists who haven't had the bad taste to become celebrities."

"Charge it to my charisma—it's a curse."

"Well, I admit you look sensational."

"Thank you, thank you!" Dietra twirled to display the purple, spangled dress she wore over red stockings. Becoming one of the more successful personalities on New

York cable TV had pushed her theatrical fashion sense to a blinding extreme. "Enough socializing," she chastised. "Time is money."

"You mean you actually learned something in film school?" Carla teased.

"Nah, from the skinflint way you run Kitchen Video. No one would ever suspect your mother was the filthy rich...oops, sorry. Anyway, time to roll—where's Billy? Ah, sweetie!" She grabbed the timid rock star and planted a red-lipstick kiss on his thin cheek. "You ready to bowl my audience over with those incredibly sexy eyes?"

This had the appropriate effect of easing his nervousness. Dietra could be an overwhelming experience for those not used to her, but she had a very potent charm. She zoomed around the set, gossiping and pattering instructions that were willingly carried out by the crew, for she also knew the technical side of her job.

Carla watched from the sidelines, amused and, as ever, impressed by her successful classmate.

The interview bubbled along effortlessly; Billy responded to Dietra's glibness with an unsuspected intelligence and sense of humor. Carla took careful note of the camera crew and the director muttering instructions from the sound-proofed booth at the rear of the ballroom. She picked up new ideas and techniques, filed them away in her voracious memory and reflected that, even if this mysterious project of Dietra's proved to be a dud, at least she would have gotten some good from the afternoon.

Dietra wrapped up the segment neatly with a rock witticism that made Billy and the crew roar with laughter. As soon as the cameras were off her, she frowned over an assistant director's clipboard and said, "Okay, you guys need me for anything more?" A loud chorus of *no*s sounded through the room. Dietra made a pouting face. "Well, jeez, you don't have to be so honest. My ego, ya know.'' Then she grabbed Carla's arm gaily and dragged her toward the door. "Bye, gang! Bye, Billy—tell your scrumptious manager I missed his pretty face on the set!'' She didn't wait for Billy's reaction.

Manager! Of course, Carla decided. The officious blond had all the hallmarks of a manager, especially that know-it-all arrogance.

"Come on, Carla!'' A tug brought Carla's thoughts back to the present. "I think there's a cheesy diner around the corner. We can talk business.''

"Good, I'm starved.''

"For food or for business?''

"Food, at least. Business is fine, I warn you.''

"Oh, I've got something I think will make your mouth water a bit.''

They settled at a window table in a café called the Old Moscow. Carla noticed that her eye kept skittering to the scene outside. She wondered who she hoped—or feared—to see. Determinedly, she concentrated on the menu.

"Oh, have the kasha and dumplings!'' Dietra insisted. "Are you still running ninety-five miles a week?''

"Twenty-five.''

"Same thing—you'll burn it off in a day, while I, alas, will have to settle for this thin, depressing salad....''

"You don't like food, Dietra. You like restaurants. We could have talked just as easily at Weeds once everyone left.''

"What a grump! Well, shall I take it you're eager to hear my proposal?''

"I'm resigned.''

"It's right up your alley, hon, no thanks to Telemusic's practice of 'art by committee.' We're doing a series of video documentaries on various jobs in the music industry—I've mentioned it, haven't I?''

''In general terms. You said you're profiling someone prominent in each of the fields.''

''Right. It's really needed doing for years. This great big popular industry, and how many of its consumers even know the difference between a promoter and a booking agent?''

''Er...I'm a little foggy on that myself.''

''For shame! With your background...''

''Hey, my mother produces *movies*, remember? There's some difference between films and rock.''

''Less and less. But I'll excuse you this time. Anyway, you know how the business is—everybody owes everybody favors. It's the same way in film, right? Well, most of the documentaries have already been handed out to the film-makers who are cozy with Telemusic's management, but I discovered that I, Dietra Sharpe, have some small amount of clout myself, and I am in charge of one whole project—managers! So show a little enthusiasm!''

Instead of enthusiasm a flutter had tickled to life in Carla's abdomen, brought on by the word *managers*. To cover it, she said, ''Remember, I'm one of those consumers who doesn't know the difference between a promoter and a booking agent.''

''Hmmm...okay, put it this way—some of these managers are bigger celebrities than their clients. Some of them wield an almost diabolical power....''

''Dietra, be straight with me. Most managers are fat, balding, little men who smoke damp cigars, right? You're only enthusiastic because you have someone particular in mind.''

Her friend sank back into her chair and screwed up one eyebrow. ''Well, yes, he *is* rather unique.''

''Who is it?'' Carla felt her jaw tighten.

"Billy's manager—Fletcher Arendt. That's why I wanted you at Weeds for the interview. I thought you might get a little glimpse of him before I told you about the project, but he didn't show. I thought seeing him might whet your appetite...what's the matter? Why do you look like you just bit down on a sourball?"

"An appropriate choice of phrasing. He *did* show."

Her lively face fell into a surprisingly sincere pout. "And I missed him? Heck..."

"Dietra, I detect more than professional enthusiasm here. You're a filmmaker, by training, anyway. Why don't *you* take a shot at this documentary? You could work with someone who had kept up on the technical progress that's been made since you last held a camera..."

"Alas, it's worse than that, Carla, hon. To tell you the truth, he's already got me marked as a lamebrain. I guess my 'media personality' makes a bad impression on some people. The only type he might even *consider* allowing to film around him would be someone obviously serious and levelheaded."

"Well," Carla replied dryly, thinking that this turn of events today was too absurd to ever use in a video, "I'm the wrong choice."

"But you *are* serious and you can be levelheaded...."

"Dietra, I punched him."

Dietra stared uncomprehendingly for a moment while Carla calmly buttered a slab of black bread and bit into it. Then she brought her hands up to cover her mouth and fell into a fit of smothered laughter.

"I'm glad *you* think it's funny. Frankly, I can't think of any more striking method of introducing myself."

Dietra wiped the tears from her eyes and gulped down some water. "Oh, Lord, Carla, you're a scream! You actually hit him? I'm not even going to ask why, I know you too well. Ha-ha-ha! Why am I laughing? My beautiful plan, my future as a TV producer, is coming down around my ears." She giggled again.

Carla sat munching, watching her friend recover, and felt a cold resolve spread through her. "Are you so sure I've blown it?"

Dietra looked surprised. "Why, aren't you?"

"Maybe, but I sure hate to let him walk free on the streets having classified you as a flake and me as a...a..."

"The word shrew comes to mind."

"Yeah, that's it." Carla raised her coffee mug in a parody of a toast. "Anyway, as I recall from film school, *you* used to be made of tougher stuff, too. The two of us made a pretty formidable team. Remember Larson's class? And what's this Fletcher Arendt anyway? Just a man."

Dietra's grin had mutated from helpless humor to something more calculating. Her brown eyes glinted with the wicked delight Carla remembered from their many escapades together long ago.

"Why, Carla, I do believe you want to do this documentary after all. What is it, his looks?"

"No, although I'll concede that he's stunning. It's his gosh-awful arrogance."

"Yay! Oh, this is going to be fun. You have no idea how I've missed doing actual video work! I mean, standing in front of a camera all day is fine but..."

"Wait a minute, wait a minute! You're going to be helping me?"

"Well, sure! You don't think I'd totally throw you to the wolves on this one, do you?"

"Give me the real reason you're so hot to get back into production."

Dietra slumped, knocked down from her extravagant enthusiasm. "Has it occurred to you, Carla, that we're getting older? We may be twenty-four now..."

"Twenty-five."

"Whatever, but if I don't get some production credits to my name, I'm going to spend the last of my youthful years on the wrong side of a camera interviewing seventeen-year-old pop stars and then have to retire at thirty. And get a *real* job."

"You're serious, aren't you?"

"Yeah. What a surprise, huh?"

"All right, I'll take you on as occasional crew. That is, if we're not jumping the gun on this."

"Good. So, shall I lay out a little background for you, partner?"

"Please. For one thing, just who does Fletcher Arendt manage? I mean, this Billy Pilgrim kid is too new. Arendt must have made his name with somebody else first."

"He did and he's still with her."

"Who?"

"Mercy Riley."

"My God, I own one of her albums. She's sort of country, right?"

"Country rock. Fletcher built up her audience there, but he's been able to broaden her popularity into rock—without losing the old fans—he's real shrewd. She's still singing about lonesome heartache and how 'he done me wrong,' but she's singing it louder and faster and her new band's got more punch. He's *real* ambitious—I hear lots of rumors these days about movie roles for her, which is part of the reason I thought of you...."

Carla tightened her voice in warning. "Dietra, as far as this video is concerned—and any others, in fact—my mother is Amelia Copeland, California housewife, *not* Amelia Abbott-Copeland of Odyssey Films. Got it?''

''Yes, ma'am. Anyway, Mercy was Fletcher's big project, his labor of love.''

''*Love* in the romantic sense?''

''No, not her. In fact, that's the really poignant part of the story you might want to bring out. See, he was an up-and-coming criminal lawyer at one time—probably pretty good background for music, come to think of it. Mercy and another girl sang in some band that was starting to go places four or five years ago. And they were *wild*! All those stories of drinking and drugs and crazy behavior you hear about musicians? That was the two of them. Then Mercy got her throat wrecked up in a car crash and the other girl got killed outright. No one ever thought Mercy would talk again, let alone sing—except Fletcher.''

''And it was the other girl he was in love with?''

''That's what they say. Makes for a pretty touching angle, doesn't it? He turns to managing the career and life of a screwup like Mercy Riley, nurses her back to health, rebuilds her confidence and keeps her out of trouble while she storms the charts. You can bet he's thinking that if he had been her manager and not just her boyfriend the other girl might still be alive. You're making a face.''

''That's so *private*, Dietra. How can you expect me to use that in some lightweight video for a rock TV station?''

Dietra looked offended. ''I didn't say it had to be lightweight. If I had wanted fluff I would have hired a Madison Avenue ad agency and it could have come out looking like a cornflakes commercial.''

''Still...''

''Everyone has motivations, Carla. No one works that hard for a prima donna singer without really deep reasons.

You've got to at least touch on them. You'll do it tastefully, I know you.''

"Well, now we come to another small obstacle, speaking of motivations. I know absolutely nothing about pop music. I spent all my teenage years synchronizing classical music to film soundtracks. I'm warped for life.''

"I'm operating on something called the 'war zone' theory. Filmmaking and, God knows, rock music are both a lot like a battlefield. I'm sending you in to live or die.'' Dietra assumed a brisk, military manner. "You'll think on your feet, you'll learn in the thick of flying bullets. You won't be trying to push stale old viewpoints—you'll be fresh and your video will be unorthodox.''

"This is hardly how you plan a coherent piece of film.''

Dietra blew out her cheeks and glared. "Shush, I'm in the grip of inspiration.''

Carla laughed heartily, already well infected with her friend's zest. It had been too long since she had been so eager to take on a project. Whether it was the project that drove the blood through her veins so wildly, or simply the chance to tackle that man again, she preferred not to consider. Everyone had motivations, indeed, but it was what they *did* that counted in the end. And she could feel an inspired piece of video waiting down the road somewhere. She was a professional, no matter what that arrogant, offensive man thought.

A few days later Carla wondered how she would ever prove her skills to Fletcher Arendt when she couldn't get close enough even to sock him again. She had written to Arendt Management; she had called Arendt Management; she had even boldly presented herself at the handsome West Fifty-seventh Street office. The walls there were hung with gold records, autographed photos of music personalities and a few amateurish woodblock prints signed "Riley." The decor was clean and arrid as a southwestern desert, with low, rope chairs, a sand-colored cotton couch, tables made of wind-shaped wood and unglazed clay pots full of cacti. The whole place smelled fresh and sweet as dried grass. Despite her nervousness, she felt a great pleasure in the surroundings.

A busy, black-haired young woman sat behind a desk of velvet-smooth oak, holding two phone conversations at once and sorting an enormous bundle of airline tickets. A little desk sign announced that her name was Annette Harrow.

Carla had groomed herself carefully, intending to look like all the adjectives that might win Arendt over: professional, rational, levelheaded, serious... Her defiant hair had been temporarily collected into a bun; only wisps of it sprang loose. The pale aqua jacket and skirt balanced summer casualness with a sense of business and, if this Arendt had remaining doubts, the case at her side held her portfolio of tapes ready to be screened.

Annette Harrow flicked Carla a look, as if to say "hang on," while she finished her phone call. "Now, Mrs. Speers, if Fletcher had made that anonymous contribution to the runaway center, he'd hardly appear on TV *admitting* that it was his, now would he?... I quite understand your position... Why don't you just ask him to appear with you as one of the *founders* of MAY? What's the date?...Ah, why that's the same day Mercy Riley will be at the MAY luncheon...Yes, what a good idea—the two of them...Yes, yes, thank you, Mrs. Speers. Good-bye." She hung up, made what could just be read as a grimace and then raised her eyebrows at Carla inquiringly. "What can I do for you?"

"I'm Carla Copeland."

"Yes?" came the noncommittal reply.

"I really must see Mr. Arendt. I'm perfectly prepared to wait as long as it takes."

The woman shrugged and let a sardonic smile curl onto her mouth. "You haven't dealt with Fletcher before then?"

Carla gritted her teeth. "Actually, I *have*—briefly."

A sympathetic look crossed the secretary's face. "Look, you're welcome to wait, but even if you talk to Fletcher you're not going to get anywhere with this video idea—it *is* a video, right? You see, we're at an incredibly busy time of the year—both our clients are starting their U.S. tours. It's keeping us jumping like a bunch of Mexican beans. And on top of that, we're moving to a new office. Fletcher's going to welcome a camera crew like he'd welcome a plague of cockroaches."

"I'm hardly a crew."

"Still...oh, go ahead, take a seat. I can see you've got that kamikaze look in your eye."

Carla sat in one of the impossibly low chairs. If Fletcher Arendt walked through the room now, she'd be at knee level.

Of course he chose that moment to emerge from his office. He came out in midsentence, dragging a phone receiver in one hand and keeping a grip on a hunk of computer printout with the other. Carla took advantage of his distraction to struggle out of the chair.

"Annette, see if we can get air cargo space between Detroit and Chicago on the fourteenth. Clayton can promise better press if we can move the Chicago gig up one day."

"Uh, Fletch..." Annette nudged her chin in Carla's direction.

Fletcher glanced up and saw her. His frown of concentration leveled out into a gaze both disapproving and oddly amused. "Come to finish me off?"

Carla fought off a flush. "In one sense or another."

Annette, frowning at her boss's familiar tone, said, "Fletcher, this is Carla Copeland who's been asking about doing that video."

"Oh yeah—Crockpot Video?"

"*Kitchen* Video," Carla corrected darkly. "Named for its location on Tenth Avenue and Forty-seventh Street."

"Ah, *Hell's* Kitchen—great place. Is that where you learned to throw a punch?"

"As a matter of fact—yes. Now, about the video..."

"I'm sorry, Ms. Copeland, there's no video. You'll have to make your home movies somewhere else."

Carla had been trying to remain sedate and reasonable, but his unprovoked sarcasm needled her. "I don't ridicule what *you* do, Mr. Arendt. Have you even read the proposal I sent you?"

"I haven't got *time* to read it, let alone to help you with your blasted video." His voice rose in exasperation.

Her voice rose further. Annette looked alarmed. "Then don't judge what you don't know anything about—just say *no!*"

"All right, I will—*no!*"

Having backed herself into this corner, Carla shut up. Fletcher looked surprised that he had felled her. He waited a long, strained moment, then demanded testily, "Go on, say something."

"Nope," Carla refused, grabbing her portfolio. "Anything else I say with my camera." With that enigmatic promise, she swung about and stormed through the outer doors.

A perplexed thoughtfulness transported Fletcher Arendt's face from its usual intense concentration. His sharp eyes drilled through the dark doors after they had closed upon Carla. He had a feeling he had somehow mishandled the last five minutes, though nothing in his experience suggested a better approach. People threw themselves at him with requests and proposals all the time; some of them pretty young women. He had found it more and more necessary to set boundaries on what could demand his attention and to let the rest take care of itself—or not. With two tours coming up and Mercy in a jealous fit over his attention to her career, those boundaries held quite enough to keep him busy. And any friend of that Dietra Sharpe's had a better than average chance of spelling trouble. Still, he felt the old rule had just failed him somehow. It didn't figure.

Annette spoke up from his elbow. "Everybody wants something, huh?"

"And lately all of them want it from *me*!" He grinned ruefully and turned back to his office where hours of work waited.

"She *was* a pretty one, wasn't she?" Annette teased.

"If you like the type."

Annette's humorous grumble reached him as he closed the office door. "Who do you think you're kidding, Fletch? *You* like the type."

Chapter Two

Fletcher Arendt called for sterner measures. Carla pondered a few on the gritty walk home through Hell's Kitchen. She had a fairly certain feeling that she couldn't trick or pressure a man like him into capitulation. He had also made it clear that persuasion through the sheer merits of her proposal was unlikely. Why couldn't she just drop it? She had a sheaf of proposals on her own worktable—requests for her services from schools and foundations, even a big ad agency wanted her to do a promotional film on playground equipment. All this opportunity sat ignored while she mulled over the exact tone of Fletcher Arendt's refusal.

That was it, wasn't it? The *tone* of his refusal. Even while the word *no* had shot from his mouth, his expression had remained expectant, humorous, almost hopeful. No, that had to be a flight of fancy on her part. He couldn't be hoping that she'd continue to pester him. . .but he did expect *something*.

Well, Carla had something to give him. When she reached the familiar warehouse on West Forty-seventh Street a small, simple plan had formed in her mind. She ran up the rickety, splintered, wooden steps, mentally ticking off a list of equipment she would need: camera, recorder, photo lamps, umbrella reflectors, tripods, cables, battery pack, color monitor, caroid microphone, and earphones. She could have gotten by with a less elaborate setup as this next little video would be seen by no more than a couple of people, but she never did shoddy work.

The equipment fit neatly into a two-wheeled trolley of her own design. The rig could be worn as a backpack, but today she only needed to roll it. She phoned for a cab and met it at the curb.

Back on the twenty-eighth floor of the marble-encrusted Fifty-seventh Street building, Carla quickly set up her portable movie set facing the motionless glass doors of Arendt Management. Many of the neighboring offices had emptied early for the start of the hot June weekend. Carla taped uninterruptedly for half an hour—an immensely boring half hour. Then she packed her rig, rewound her tape cartridge and slipped a note inside the case that read: "Dear Mr. Arendt, The enclosed tape is my documentary in-progress on Arendt Management. Due to your level of input, this is the tape that will be presented to Telemusic. You are the one to judge whether I have captured the operation accurately, or as you wish it to be portrayed. If you have any additions or corrections, please call. Carla Copeland/Kitchen Video."

Then she marched in to the desk of the impassive Annette, handed her the tape and dragged the trolley back home.

It should have worked. It should have provoked *some* reaction. Carla fidgeted through that night and all day Saturday, wondering if the next telephone call would bring her Fletcher Arendt's voice—even if it was angry. Was the man made of stone? Then she remembered the lively interest in his eyes all through each of their two confrontations. He did not follow any standard behavior, no matter how she had criticized him that first time. He seemed to constantly take in and evaluate his situation, and to respond in his own individual way. A man like that was sensitive. If he had run her video by now, he'd be having *some* reaction. She was wild to know what it was.

Although it was a useless gesture, she called Dietra to report on her lack of progress. Dietra did not sound surprised.

"He's a hard case, isn't he?"

"Slippery. I feel like I'm groping around in cloudy water for a fish. I know he's there. I get little tickles of current once in a while, but I can't get a grip."

"That's your problem, Carla, you keep trying to play fair. If you were starving would you splash around in a stream giving the darn fish an even chance? No! You'd get a net."

"If he were a fish. And if I were starving."

"Well, *I'm* starving!" Dietra declared. "Remember my advancing age, Carla."

"So what's the next step?"

"Hmmm...Well, I've got one in mind, but it's not what you'd call subtle."

"I'm not surprised."

Dietra's hesitation aroused Carla's apprehension, especially when she said, "Let me work on this myself, Carla. It's not really your style."

"Wait a minute..."

"Look, if you want one last confrontation with him, I know where he'll be tonight—there's a party at Chevrons for the backers of a new movie production company. You'll be right at home. He's feeling out some opportunities for Mercy's new career. With your mother's name you'll have no trouble getting in.''

"You know what I think of that idea.''

"If you want this project, you'll use whatever advantages you've got on your side. So get yourself on that guest list and go!''

"And you're going to do *what*?'' Carla tried to sound commanding, even though she knew Dietra would pay no attention.

"Trust me—if you don't know, no one can blame you, right?''

It hardly served to point out that those two sentences didn't make sense together. Carla felt true alarm. "Dietra! Wait!'' The line went dead. Carla rubbed her forehead in annoyance. Dietra might be perfectly willing to accept responsibility for some unimaginably rash act, but Carla suspected it would not be Dietra who intercepted the first blow of reaction.

With a sense of stern fatality, Carla dug through her musty address book and located an old colleague of her mother's. The woman sounded astonished to hear from Carla, as if she felt she was talking to someone who had returned from the grave, but she was happy to help. Within minutes she had opened one of the most jealously guarded doors in the industry and secured an invitation to the party at Chevrons. Carla could have spent her life at trendy clubs such as this one, drinking, flirting and talking film. She preferred to *make* film, and only for that reason, ironically, would she endure Chevrons tonight.

Well, maybe for one other reason, too....

That evening she stood in the center of the rag rug that defined her bedroom in the corner of the big studio, and tore item after item out of the clothes cupboard. Her life did not include a lot of jet-set parties; she was rather short of fizzy outfits. A sudden inspiration caused her to giggle. Of course! You didn't wear an outfit to these things—you wore a *costume*. On the opposite end of her studio she kept trunks of props. An amazing variety of garbage accumulated from just a few years of filmmaking. She wistfully fingered a huge black velvet cape lined in red satin before pushing it aside. It always came as a shock to her to realize she was only five-foot-two and petite and couldn't get away with such dramatic outfits. She felt like a warrior.

Ah, here now! She pulled out a scrap of peacock-blue silk and examined it carefully. The smell of camphor nearly knocked her over. She hung the dress by an open window and went to dig out her fabric steamer.

The finished effect satisfied her. The dress was simply two squares of heavy silk sewn together, with gaps left for head and limbs; consequently, it slid off her shoulder whenever she moved. But the shoulder didn't look half bad and the body revealed by the sweeps of floating, knee-length silk was slender and well conditioned. She didn't need any girdles to keep it in line.

Her eyes picked up the green of the silk and, giving in to a tiny burst of vanity, she lined them with dark gold. She would never manage the seductive sophistication that was in style, but she knew she had a delicate, elfin quality that some men found attractive. She wondered if Fletcher Arendt would, then squelched the thought. That was *not* how Carla Copeland got jobs.

She slipped on stockings and little silver-heeled sandals, fluffed her hair into its fullest mane, and called for a taxi. For one of her meager income, she spent a great deal of time being chauffeured. She reckoned that if her video career ever came to naught, she could certainly write a consumers' guide to taxi service in Manhattan.

Chevrons occupied four floors of a town house in the fashionable neighborhood near Lincoln Center. When Carla stepped out of her cab she attracted the attention of a crowd of celebrity-watchers. They clearly could not figure out who she was to be able to breeze so easily past the officious bouncer.

The blast of dance music hit Carla in the face like a boxing glove. The main level of the club was a sea of moving bodies tangled by the swirling, pulsing lights. The chaos made her almost nauseous. Obeying her dim memories of one other party she reluctantly had attended here, she headed for a glass-enclosed elevator that slid slowly between the floors.

The second level up held a video room. Three big screens rained down flickering images from old movies. No one on the floor paid much attention. Level three appeared to be a games parlor stocked with pinball, video games, pool tables and shuffleboards, which people played in a bored manner.

She stepped off onto the top level into a scene that looked surprisingly like a normal cocktail party. Murmuring voices and clinking glasses provided most of the sounds, though the dance beat still reverberated through the floor. Low white settees and slender, white-stemmed trees in chrome-banded pots created little alcoves of privacy. Two bars done in a quiet Art-Deco simplicity flanked the room, and a wall of glass looked out over the dark tranquillity of Central Park.

Carla slipped into the space between two trees and glanced over the scene. She had been out of her mother's sphere for years now, in college and as an independent; the chances of meeting anyone who recognized her were not *huge,* but she dreaded the very possibility. She'd worked hard at being simply Carla Copeland. On the west coast it was impossible, due to her mother's prominence. If she jinxed New York, she would have run out of coasts.

She quickly spied her quarry. It wasn't just his snow-white suit that showed so vividly against the shadows, it was the vitality that animated his tall, broad-shouldered form and glowed through his golden skin. She well understood Dietra's fascination with Fletcher Arendt, and her choice of him for the documentary. Regardless of his other credentials, his hot, tawny beauty would light up a film like an image of the sun.

"Don't overdramatize," Carla warned herself in an inaudible mumble. "He's only a man."

As if he had heard her cautionary remark, Fletcher Arendt looked up and pinned her with a stare that scorched through her every slumbering nerve. It was as precise and barbed as an arrow. She teetered on her shoes. With a short word, he disengaged himself from those around him and started walking toward her. He had one hand thrust into a pocket, brushing the white jacket back from a yellow silk shirt and white tie. He walked like a lion considering prey, almost lazy, yet edgy with power. She braced herself unconsciously, and started at the sight of the scrawny figure who had just come into view behind Fletcher. It was Morey Leyland, a screwball who liked to put up money for movies and then try to get his hand in the directing. Her mother would no longer work with him, no matter how much money he had. Unfortunately he had been a fixture on the set of at least one Odyssey production while Carla had been in high school. He might *just* recognize her....

She ducked stealthily through the potted trees, annoyed that Fletcher would probably think she had done it to escape him. Well, her luck with him had been loathsomely bad so far, why improve it?

At the bar she ordered a bourbon on ice, more to give her hand something to hold than for courage. She had never lacked courage; in fact, in her younger days people had told her she was a bit reckless and overemotional. She had tried to correct this, with only partial success.

She wondered morosely what awkward mess she'd find herself in, what Dietra might have done over the hours since they had talked. The possibilities boggled the mind. Dietra had no reputation for sense.

A husky voice at her ear made her nearly choke on her drink. "I thought for a minute there, after I saw your little video, that beneath that bad temper you might have a sense of humor. I guess I was wrong."

She slowly twisted her head to look at him; he had walked soundlessly to within half a foot of her ear and she found herself close enough to see the individual amber lashes that flared from his copen-blue eyes. He was even taller than she remembered, tall enough to cast her in deep shadow despite the heels she wore.

She didn't know what he referred to, but was determined not to ask. She'd let him reveal himself; she'd cloak herself in enigmatic silence until his own talk betrayed exactly what Dietra had done. To this end she swiveled entirely, turning the maneuver into a negligent stretch, and leaned carelessly on the bar rail. In this way she gave herself a few more inches of distance from his smiling face. She hated to admit it, but those few inches helped her head to remain clear.

"You have no remarks? No apologies? Threats?" he inquired curiously.

"Not at the moment."

His dark eyebrows slid upward in an expression resembling disappointment. Then, to her surprise, he nodded brusquely and walked away.

This was not in the plan. Grimly, she followed him across the party floor and into a screen of trees that carved out a pocket of privacy next to the windowed wall. His white suit and fair hair were luminous against the rare blackness of park and sky. The strip of city lights from the tall buildings on the opposite side of the park made a sparkling frame for him. Though he attended closely to the lighting of a cigarette, he seemed well aware of her as she closed in. She planted herself in front of him and put her hands firmly on her hips, as if the pose might add to her size. "For your information, I *have* a sense of humor. In particular, I have a great sense of the ridiculous, or else I wouldn't still be trying to snag you for this infernal video!"

"Infernal!" he repeated. "I like the sound of that. Do you see me as Lucifer, then? Will you show me ruling in my little hell of rock and roll? I like this idea."

Ignoring his sarcasm, she persisted. "Enough to do the video?"

"No. A devil has his pride, Ms. Copeland. I could hardly let you seem to bully me into this."

Bully. Here was a clue—Dietra had done something heavy-handed, spoken to someone, made some kind of a deal.... Carla pressed for more information. "Couldn't you just see it as the desperate act of an inspired filmmaker? Sort of snatching a great idea from the jaws of oblivion?" The metaphors came out more mangled than clear. Fletcher made a face of similarly mangled disbelief and disgust. Carla tried again. "All right, don't look at it from my point of view. After all, why should you care if together we create a little gem of film history, a crystallization of the essense of music melded to video—it's nothing to you." One of his eyebrows had wheeled up like a gull on the wind. "But think of the free publicity you'll be getting for Mercy and Billy—all that time on Telemusic, the most popular rock cable station in the northeast. You can't *buy* time like that."

"This thas been put to me before, as you obviously know, by someone with a much keener grasp of the business than I imagine you have, Ms. Copeland. And the answer is still no."

She stamped her foot, wishing she had on an army boot to give the gesture more impact. Instead, the stubby little needle heel of her sandal jabbed the carpet, making no sound whatsoever. It was infuriating. She took it out on Fletcher. "You're pretty damn secure, aren't you, Mr. Arendt? You don't need anyone's help, you don't need to cooperate with the rest of the world—or even with somebody who's virtually a colleague in your own field. It must be great living up on Mount Olympus like that. I hope you never get blown off." She knew she'd be amazed in retrospect at the hotheaded statements she had made with so little provocation. Right then words hardly seemed adequate to throw at this impassive, cold-eyed man.

With chilling control he replied, "If I'm anywhere, Ms. Copeland, it's because I worked to get there, not because I've made some clumsy attempt to pull strings with record companies...."

Pulling strings with record companies? Carla's mind raced. That sounded like something Dietra would try. A quick retort sprang to her lips. "You hardly give me the *chance* to work, Mr. Arendt. And besides, if I decided to start pulling strings, I could do a lot better than..." She snapped her mouth shut. What a vexing man! She hadn't been so careless in a long time.

Fletcher Arendt regarded her quizzically, his curiosity obviously pricked by her chopped-off threat. Just as he seemed to be taking a breath to demand an explanation, Carla found rescue from an unlikely source. An exquisitely pretty young woman, the buxom starlet type, wafted up to Fletcher on a rustle of red tulle. Her eyes passed appraisingly over Carla and, evidently finding her of little significance, fixed their dewy gaze on Fletcher. To Carla's disgust, if not to her surprise, he softened; his smile seemed genuinely warm.

"Fletcher, you magnificent man, here you are hiding behind the trees," she breathed seductively. Carla hadn't heard a conversation start off like that since she had left California. "Could you do me the teeniest, tiniest favor?" The starlet creature swayed against Fletcher with both hands draped over his broad shoulders and her nose practically buried in his hair.

"You know I'd do anything for you, Elizabeth."

She graced him with a smile so intimate that it caused Carla to writhe, and then she murmured inaudibly into his attentive ear.

"Why, of course," he replied softly. "Just come up to the office and Annette can dig it out for you."

Elizabeth arranged her delicately glossed lips into a pout. "Won't you be there, Fletcher? I'd like to thank you in person."

"Hmmm. . .you might just find me in—mornings are best—they're quieter."

As if to seal this private pact, the woman kissed him lingeringly on the cheek and drifted off. Carla counted the seconds until his attention returned to her. "Well," she said significantly. "*That* was instructive. I see not everyone has a hard time with you."

His eyes narrowed to glacier-blue slits, keen and daunting. "Be careful what you say next, Ms. Copeland. You *could* learn something from that young lady. For instance, how to make yourself pleasant even when you want a favor.''

Carla glared fire. ''I'm fairly certain *her* methods wouldn't suit me.''

A mischievous grin played with the corners of his mouth and slanted eyes. ''Afraid you couldn't compete?'' He reached over and snubbed out his cigarette in an ashtray on the window ledge. She saw in the gesture a deceptive negligence, a laziness that disguised something very deliberate and assured.

Of course he had understood her innuendo and replied with his own suggestion that she might be sexually lacking. Trying to look arch, she declared, ''No one has ever had any complaints.''

''I prefer to judge for myself,'' came the reply. As she tried to grasp his meaning, his eyes bore down on hers. He was close enough that she could see the individual strands of his spun-gold hair turned silver by the lights and could smell the mingled scent of tobacco and musk that tantalized the air around him. How had he gotten this close? Her feet refused to let her retreat, even as he gathered her into his arms.

He gave her a sneaky, unrelenting kiss, just rough enough to startle her, then, while her defenses were down, to capture the most protected depths of her mouth. Roused enough to struggle, she merely succeeded in tightening his arms behind her back. His teeth stung her lips, his tongue filled her with a shocked awareness of the power of the man whose heart beat against her breasts.

Finally regaining some of her control, she wrestled one hand free and pushed it against his throat. He immediately released her, but his hands kept their grip upon her arms until she found her own balance. She couldn't think over the clamor of her emotions. He regarded her speechlessness with open amusement.

"Well, I finally found something that will shut you up." Then he calmly lit another cigarette.

Shock still hindered Carla's reaction—shock at his presumption and at her own inadequate response. She should have killed him by now. "Was *that* what all this was about?"

"Ms. Copeland, since we met a few days ago you have hit me, criticized me in front of my business associates, threatened me with a bad joke and with pressure from Mercy's record company, accused me of being smug *and* of being a lecher. You drive a man awfully hard! Considering what I'd *like* to do to you, I think I've behaved very well." He put on an exaggeratedly pathetic expression that tickled her even as she fumed.

She mentally pulled back, to consider what he had just said from a longer perspective. He had a point. The poor man had never heard of her or her video until a few days ago. She had pursued him with the same fervor and lack of consideration as the paparazzi who hid in bushes to photograph stars. She had responded to his polite refusals with temper and recrimination. How much of this would she have put up with herself?

Chastened, Carla composed herself. Her outrage evaporated and a cool, rational light illuminated her thoughts. "You're right, Mr. Arendt. I wouldn't want to work with someone who acted as I have this past week either." She put out her hand. "I hope you'll accept my apologies. I won't trouble you again."

He took her hand, wordless now in his turn. Before she could stumble into any more bad behavior, she turned and left the party.

The next day Carla planted herself at her worktable and began weeding with grim purpose through her stack of options. She hoped that this past week had simply been an aberration in her behavior, possibly caused by...by what? Bizarre personal chemistry with Fletcher Arendt? He did seem to bring out the worst in her. No, not the worst—more like the *extreme,* for while she had found her temper chafed absolutely raw around him, she had also found her enthusiasm for the darned video constant and compelling. It would have been grand to work in such an intensified state and with such a singular man. None of these proposals before her caused more than a flutter of interest, but she must pick one anyway. The very force of her reactions warned her away from Fletcher Arendt. He had gotten to her on much too deep a level, dangerously close to the private Carla, whom she kept away from the claws of her professional world.

At midmorning the phone rang. Carla's hand involuntarily hesitated over the receiver; she had an inexplicable impression that she was putting her fingers to a hot stove. She drove away the feeling and answered.

"Ms. Copeland," said a familiar, husky voice. A wave of heat blew through her like a savanna wind. "This is Fletcher Arendt. I've been mulling over this video idea since we last spoke."

Carla nearly choked. He chose such a delicate way of putting it. "Yes?"

"I think we may be able to work together." He paused, apparently waiting for some comment from her. When he continued his tone was gently chiding, tinged with humor. "Ms. Copeland, you can't imagine that you're the only one capable of sudden changes in outlook. I wouldn't be serving my clients well if I didn't let the occasional new idea creep into my dull brain, now would I?"

Her amazement had started to recede, exposing her own humor. "What won you over—the sheer brilliance of my vision?"

"Not exactly."

"Then what?"

"Actually, your brilliance will be a happy little bonus to my plan. Let me explain—you've probably heard that my client Mercy Riley has been considering branching out into films...."

Carla's insides froze like cubes in an ice tray. Oh, no, he must have found out about old Odyssey Films somehow and was about to press her into service as a contact, wheedle favors out of her in exchange for video rights.... What else could have caused such an abrupt change of heart?

"Ms. Copeland!" came an unexpected exclamation.

"Huh?"

"I heard you inhale and then nothing. Are you all right?"

"Yes," she replied frostily. "Please go on."

"I've decided that your doing a video around me will be a good opportunity to teach Mercy the nuts and bolts of the business. She won't then walk onto her own first set a total novice. I want you to work with her as you film—explain what you're doing, the equipment you're using, let her into your studio or lab or wherever you process your film..."

"Tape," she corrected feeling almost stunned with relief. "It's videotape—it doesn't need to be processed, just edited. There are some major technical and procedural differences between film and tape."

"But you can explain them to her as you go?"

"Oh sure, I know both fields. Hasn't she ever made any of those promotional videos?"

"No. Until recently she had a low-key, country audience. It's the rock audience that insists on videos. We've just finished Billy's second, so it's old hat to him, but Mercy's only done TV appearances, and they've been large productions and the people were too busy to work with her. Are you willing to take on a student?''

Carla carefully quelled the rush of excitement she felt and asked, ''Will I have access to all areas of your work?''

''I can't make quite such a blanket promise—some situations are more ticklish than others. We'll have to work them out one by one. But I *do* promise you'll have my sincere cooperation. Is that good enough?''

''Yes.'' She had a feeling that it was quite a bit better than just ''good enough.''

''Fine. We're meeting Mercy at the airport this morning. I'll pick you up around eleven-fifteen—look for a gray limo with a license plate that reads 'MUSIC.' ''

''Mr. Arendt, let me assure you there will be no *other* gray limousines on my block.''

Fletcher chuckled and sounded satisfied when he hung up. She sat by the phone breathing deeply to keep her head clear. Excitement was fine, natural, she told herself. But more than ever she had to be the complete professional: brisk, calm, sharp, cooperative. Fletcher Arendt would never regret giving her this chance—nor ever know how it caused her heart to pound.

Chapter Three

The poker-faced chauffeur bundled Carla and her thirty pounds of equipment into the backward-facing seat of a long gray car. Fletcher sat opposite on the dark gray suede rear seat, separated from her by a wide expanse of thickly carpeted floor. The sight of his bright corona of hair and shrewd, relentless eyes seemed to shrink the distance between them to nothing. Even now, in the clear light of day, with her resolve firmly pulled around her, Carla felt the bite of his power—the magnetism that had immediately drawn her gaze last night at Chevrons. She had tried determinedly not to think about her softheaded reaction to his kiss. He had only meant it as a shock tactic. No matter how galvanizing his effect, she had to make sure it worked on *videotape*, not on *her*.

"Good morning, Mr. Arendt," she said pleasantly as soon as she had stashed her rig where it wouldn't fall.

"Oh, call me Fletcher, *please*—you get used to a certain amount of casualness in this business. I might not remember to answer to 'Mr. Arendt.' And I'll be so bold as to call you Carla, all right?"

She nodded. After all, he had been bolder. Pretending to adjust a strap on the trolley, she studied him from beneath her lashes. The crisp white suit of Chevrons had been replaced by faded jeans over his long, solidly muscled legs. A light navy jacket kept out the chill of the limo's air conditioning and a red bandana made a splash of color against the open collar of his pale blue shirt. The sunlight fell brightly on burnished-gold skin and made his eyes reflect amber sparks. His gaze ran over her like a tongue of electricity and she dropped her eyes back to the equipment.

"May I begin?" she asked with a little too much briskness.

"Of course. I never like to waste time myself." He meant this literally. Fascinated, Carla forgot her own preparations as she watched him set up a miniature office right there on the seat. A phone appeared from behind the sliding panel in the car door, his attaché case proved to contain file folders, a tape recorder and a tiny computer.

Recovering, Carla extended the cord that connected her camera to the recorder in her backpack. The light mounted above her lens, meant to brighten the eyes of a subject in close-up, added a little illumination to the car's interior, but she'd have to rely on the sunlight that filtered in through the windows. This video would definitely have a rough-and-ready quality to it—war zone, indeed!

Fletcher could have been a field commander checking the disposition of his forces over a broad and complex terrain. With utter concentration and efficiency he dealt with item after item on a ten-page list already marked in multiple colors. He placed a string of phone calls—confirming appointments, pressing for information and commitments, following the progress of more projects than Carla could sort out in her mind.

He seemed to be constantly untangling answers from a bramble of legal-sounding double-talk. Eventually Carla realized he was, in large part, checking on the last-minute details for a concert Mercy Riley seemed to be giving at Radio City Music Hall the next evening for something called MAY. For fifteen minutes he quizzed the promoter on ticket sales, security, sound checks, union clearances, space on the loading dock, press coverage and on and on.

Carla had struggled with the logistics of three and four camera movies involving up to twenty-five people in cast and crew. The amount of detail loaded into each had stricken her with nervous tremors for weeks during filming. The picture she was now piecing together of Fletcher's efforts suggested something much larger. Yet he had agreed to add *her* to his mountain of worries. Impressed, she watched him work, no trace of strain marring his expressive face.

The limo took the mangled city streets in its well-cushioned stride and crossed the Manhattan Bridge onto the slightly smoother Brooklyn-Queens Expressway. Carla propped her camera lens on the door ledge, silently thanking the professor who had made her learn how to hold a camera steady by having her practice on rides at an amusement park. She taped the skyline of Lower Manhattan, she taped the cruising traffic, the back of the chauffeur's head, anything that might help her get across information or create a mood later during editing. Mostly she taped Fletcher. Dietra, for all her aggravating maneuvers, had given her an extremely photogenic subject—and one not a bit camera shy. She taped and he worked.

The limo passed all the usual exits for Kennedy Airport, finally turning down one that took them over a desolate stretch of concrete past cargo terminals and unlabeled hangars. Planes taxied along runways so close Carla could feel the heavy thrum of their engines through the body of the car. The driver stopped beside a long line of tiny private planes tethered to the ground by wires.

Fletcher opened the door, peered out, checked his watch and said to the driver, "Right on time. Remind me to give the pilots a nice Christmas present." Then he jumped out.

Carla dove after him, settling the camera in her shoulder brace so she could tape on the run. Fletcher must have had eyes like an eagle's—it took her a full minute to locate the tiny white jet skimming along through the heat haze. The jet slowed, turned to follow some guidelines painted on the runway and taxied toward them.

Fletcher waited until it was about a hundred yards away and then dashed over in time to put his hand up to a woman who stepped from the door onto the wing. Carla zoomed in and recognized Mercy Riley—her new pupil. That head of burnt-chestnut hair had been on enough album and magazine covers to make itself instantly familiar. Fletcher lifted her off the wing as if she had no weight, although it became clear that she was a tall woman and blessed with a figure that made Carla feel like a scrawny child.

Mercy shifted in Fletcher's welcoming embrace until they were arm in arm. She chattered gaily as they walked back toward the limo and Fletcher listened with an easy smile softening his face.

"Fletcher, honey," Mercy drawled in an ambling southern accent. "I'm not sure I like this arriving in secrecy business—it's too *secret*!"

"I know, but I couldn't afford to risk your getting tied up at the airport with fans and newsmen. You've got interviews back to back at the hotel, every hour on the hour, and a press conference at eight. This benefit concert is pulling in a lot of publicity for MAY.''

Mercy sighed sadly and her huge blue, cinnamon-lashed eyes lit on Carla for the first time. ''Home movies, Fletcher? Why, I'm touched.''

''Mercy Riley, this is Carla Copeland. She's doing a documentary on the music business, so she'll be part of the circus for a while.''

Carla noticed that he carefully skirted the fact that the documentary featured *him;* presumably his star had a delicate ego. Carla dutifully played her part. ''I'll be very glad to explain the work as we go along, Ms. Riley. Fletcher tells me you're becoming quite involved in filmmaking yourself. I hope I can be of help.''

The only gratification she found for that mealymouthed bit of garbage was Fletcher's look of approval. Mercy's response had a sullen, suspicious cast to it and her words went no further than ''I see.'' Then she slid bonelessly into the limo. Fletcher waited for Carla to precede him, murmuring in a just-audible voice as she passed, ''Very good, Fellini.''

The ride back into Manhattan taxed Carla's patience. She taped a few seconds of Fletcher and Mercy together on the backseat, until Mercy's glare discouraged her. The singer seemed neither interested in learning anything nor in being taped. Eventually Carla laid the camera down and resorted to her notebook, writing down ideas on possible shots, questions to ask Fletcher, errands to do to keep her private life together. She felt so invisible she wondered if Fletcher even remembered she was there. He spent the whole ride coaching Mercy on her appearances and interviews scheduled for the next several days.

At the posh Parkside Hotel in Manhattan the doorman and clerks fawned over Mercy; the manager greeted her with a bouquet of yellow roses and she sparkled with charm, evidently recovered from the disappointment of arriving in secret.

Camera hanging from her shoulder, trolley dragging across the lush carpet, Carla tagged along into the gorgeous suite of rooms Fletcher had engaged for his star. Flowers gushed from vases on every sill and tabletop. Their scent lay heavy and sweet on the air.

"Why, Fletcher! Wherever did you find white lilacs?" Mercy sighed.

His pure blue eyes opened in exaggerated innocence. "What makes you think it was me? Your admirers are beyond number."

Mercy swirled and tickled him under the chin with a sprig of blossoms. "Fletcher," she cooed, "I know you too well and beneath that rawhide skin of yours you are hopelessly sentimental. By the way, did my bags make it to the hotel?"

"They came early this morning—they're in your room. And the ones that didn't fit are in a warehouse on the West Side."

She swatted him with the sprig. "Costumes, honey. My fans expect a certain standard of glamour, you know."

"Your costumes for the tour are still at Adrian Macklin's waiting for your final fitting day after tomorrow."

"Oh you *are* so literal. I mean costumes for parties and such. I can't wear a suede cowgirl dress to dinner with the president of my record company, can I? Even if he is that detestable Bob Rhoades. Well, I'm just dying for a little soak in a big tub." So saying, she disappeared through the door to an adjoining room.

"First interview in an hour and a quarter," Fletcher called after her.

"Yes, yes," came the unconcerned answer.

"Annette will be here to throw out anyone who overstays his welcome or gives you a hard time."

Mercy reappeared in the doorway, half undressed and not in the least self-conscious. She said accusingly, "You're deserting me, Fletcher?"

"For a couple of hours. The kid's in the last stage of rehearsals for his tour. You know he needs moral support."

Mercy's lower lip swelled petulantly. "*I* need it too."

Fletcher's eyebrows straightened to an inflexible line across his forehead. Carla thought she could sense the very air darken. "Mercy," he said warningly. "We've been over this before."

The singer glared, but her sharp gaze fell, blunted by Fletcher's determination. "I wouldn't dream of keeping you from your work." She whirled away with a snap of her long, loose hair and presently the sound of bathwater washed through the uncomfortable silence.

Fletcher shook his golden head, but betrayed no other trace of displeasure. Carla realized with sudden clarity how much generosity he had shown in taking *her* on, another tempestuous female, as far as he could see. She renewed her vow of reasonableness.

"Come on, Fellini," he said, apparently undimmed. "Let's go see how the other half lives."

Fletcher had meant that remark literally—Billy's rehearsal hall was a dark, echoing warehouse in the alleys of Lower Manhattan—quite a contrast to the Parkside's gilt opulence. But the next few hours were much more to Carla's liking than the previous ones in Mercy Riley's fractious company. Billy clearly saw Fletcher as some ideal older brother and the camaraderie between manager and band was endearing.

Fletcher, thus far the stern, patriarchal figure, loosened up and showed a boyish side as he pitched in to help with the rehearsal. He wrestled amplifiers and taped cables to the rough wooden floor; his face cracked into a delicious grin, his eyes gleamed, his hair ruffled into frosty blond waves. Carla could well imagine that, after days of nonstop business negotiations, this might well seem like play to him.

Holding him in the viewfinder as he jumped around would have taxed Carla's abilities to the limit, but it was bad lighting that kept her from picking up her camera. A stubborn part of her mind insisted on plotting camera angles and editorial cuts. Too much great material was slipping away. She needed help. Annette's words loomed in her mind, "Fletcher's going to welcome a camera crew like he'd welcome a plague of cockroaches." She *needed* a crew, or at least help.

She'd have to brave it. Fortified with a vision of herself looking somehow tall and substantial, a businesswoman, rather than a waif in jeans, she went in search of Fletcher. She only found him when he spoke unexpectedly over the top of her head.

"Enjoying yourself, Fellini?"

Startled, she looked up and saw him stretched full length across the top of a six-foot-high amp crate, as relaxed as a lion on a sunny ledge. He shifted seamlessly from one persona to another—from calculating businessman to affectionate colleague to this lazy Huck Finn. She sensed that each was a genuine part of a many-faceted character.

"Actually, I feel like I'm doing you a great disservice by not taping in here," she began diplomatically.

"Then why aren't you?"

"Two reasons—the lighting is very poor. I'm afraid any tape would look like it was done underwater. And second, there's too much activity to capture with just one camera."

"Sorry I don't have a sound stage handy."

"Oh, I can *make* a sound stage—just a few well-placed lights and reflectors..."

"And sixteen assistants scrambling around underfoot?"

She had the feeling he was needling her. "*One* would be enough."

"Go to it, Fellini. I don't want a second-rate job out of this."

A tiny prickle of annoyance hit her. She was trying to be considerate, after all.

Fletcher watched her through razor-slit eyes. "I am a reasonable man, *really*," he pointed out and jumped fluidly down from the crate, leaving her to fume unobserved.

Shrugging herself free of aggravation, Carla found a telephone and called Dietra.

The TV star sounded groggy when she answered.

"Your hour of glory is upon you," Carla announced briskly. "The video world calls."

"Use simple English, please."

"I need your camera-toting body on my set for several hours."

"You mean you expect me to jump around under eighty pounds of electronics? This poor thin body that just crawled into bed a few minutes ago?...Wait a minute—you've called *me*, does that mean Fletcher Arendt agreed to the documentary?"

"It does, although you did an almost perfect job of jinxing it with your stupid maneuver of calling Mercy Riley's record company. That *is* what you did, isn't it?"

"Well, yeah, I might have mentioned it to Bob Rhoades..."

Carla cut her off. "Well, I managed to snatch victory from the jaws of defeat, but we'll have to have a serious discussion about tactics in the near future, partner. To say nothing of ethics.''

''How is Fletcher to work with?''

''Oh, he's fine,'' Carla conceded. She peered between aisles of mammoth crates and watched the character in question tenderly replacing an audio pickup on Billy's guitar. He was somewhat more than *fine*. In the rising heat of the afternoon he had stripped off his jacket and shirt, and the skin over his powerful arms and shoulders gleamed like polished oak. She dragged her attention to the dull black phone. ''Now take this down.'' She dictated to Dietra a list of spots and floodlights, monitors, filters, a video mixer for the two-camera setup, microphones, and audio recording equipment. Dietra repeated the list and meekly agreed to be there within the hour. Then Carla called her landlord Gino and told him to let Dietra in.

Surprisingly, Dietra made it in an hour, proving her determination to get back in touch with production work. During one of the band's breaks, the two women strung lights and cables and plotted shot sequences. When the band went back to work Carla and her eager helper taped smoothly for two hours, so well-coordinated they didn't need to try and confer above the roar of amplified guitars.

Their tape ran out and the band wrapped up at the same time. Carla happily stacked away four cassettes of lively camera work, much of it concentrated on Fletcher as he had closely followed the rehearsal, dashed to fix loose guitar straps, hung over the soundboard, and made cryptic notes in his ever-present notebook. Carla felt pleased; she also felt as if she had run ten miles over hard rocks. A hot shower and a quiet dinner seemed the greatest reward the world could offer for such labor. She only let herself look weary to Dietra. Around Fletcher, if she couldn't manage to actually sparkle, she pulled off a fairly energetic calm.

"Look at him," Dietra groaned, wiping damp curls off her forehead. "He's ready to go on all night. A normal mortal would have at least sat down to rest at this point."

Fletcher still strode back and forth in the studio, checking lists and instructions with each worn-out musician. When he passed Carla on his rounds he announced energetically, "The limo will be back in half an hour to take us to Mercy's press conference. Afraid you'll have to handle taping by yourself, Carla, it'll be quite crowded." So saying, he jaunted off.

Carla exchanged incredulous looks with Dietra. "Press conference? Dietra, have you got any vitamin B_{12} on you?"

"Boy, when he decides to give you access, he really means it! Still, *I* wouldn't turn up my nose at a couple more hours with him!"

"You would if you already felt as if you'd been run over by a truck."

"So tell him. He seems cooperative with *you*."

"Never! I'm playing Superwoman in this story. Remember that, Dietra—there must be no suggestion that I might fall over dead during the project—or that I might get mad either."

"Why not?"

"Because I think all this bonhomie is a test. He's already seen me with my bad temper flying in the wind and it *wasn't* what encouraged him to agree to the video. I think he'd half like to crack me."

Dietra gazed wistfully after the busy, bronzed form. "Well," she sighed. "I know I'd like to crack him. You notice he still seems to think I'm beneath contempt."

"Nah, he's just preoccupied, that's all. Speaking of which, we'd better hurry and tear down the lights quick before the limo comes or you'll get stuck doing all the drudge work by yourself."

"I don't mind," declared Dietra stoutly and she promptly furled an umbrella reflector. Gallant as her friend was proving, Carla knew a TV personality probably lacked the hardened muscles needed for the work. Carla had better tackle the worst of it herself. They had ringed the rehearsal space with diffuse floods to soften the harshest shadows. These hung from any rafter she and Dietra had been able to reach with their slim choice of climbing equipment.

Carla clambered up a stack of small crates onto one of the giant amp cases and reached out for the nearest flood. The clip was stiff and she had to lean far out into the open space to jiggle it. While she worked, she heard an awful burst of swearing by a deep, rough voice, and felt the crates jar heavily beneath her knees. Her delicate balance destroyed, she gasped sharply and reached for the rafter. In the next second an arm clamped about her waist and threw her flat on top of the hard, black crate. With the breath knocked out of her, she could only stare up into Fletcher's blazing face. His long legs were tangled with hers, and much of his weight lay solidly on her right hip. He kept her pinned between his arms as if she could not be trusted loose.

"Do you have a death wish?" he demanded.

She managed to remember she was supposed to be calm and reasonable, so her reply was delivered in as controlled a tone of voice as she could manage with her lungs crushed. "Do you think you're Errol Flynn?" A tentative wiggle toward freedom was cut short by the tightening of his arms along her sides.

"Don't talk back. Someone with as little sense as you have should be very cautious of opening her mouth."

Remain calm, Carla reminded herself. "Fletcher, I know you're in the habit of *taking care* of people, but I do know what I'm doing." She watched as his furious eyes darkened into somber thought—she sensed she had touched some important depth in him. "I run and do weight-training just so I *can* climb around like this."

His eyes opened wide and she saw that the pupils had constricted in alarm, making the blue of his irises even more startling. His eyebrows and lashes weren't really so dark, after all; their shadowy color was shot with gold.

"I don't care if you have a pilot's license! Unless you grow *wings*, don't ever try anything like that again!"

Carla was increasingly anxious to be let up and to get some distance between herself and this overwhelming man. The imperative pressure of his body on hers was driving away her steadiness. Soon she knew she would say something caustic. She gritted her teeth. "Thank you for being concerned. I'll try not to do anything chancy from now on, okay?"

Still glaring, Fletcher let her up. She scrambled off the crate with what competence she could muster. The experience of being flat on her back, thigh to thigh with him had rattled her more than she cared to admit.

From the top of the case, Fletcher watched her with eyes that could have bored holes in wood. Truly ignoring him would be impossible—she'd settle for the appearance, and so walked placidly over to Dietra and began pulling electrician's tape off the floor in satisfyingly loud rips.

Head down, Dietra whispered, "Gee, I wish that had been me up there."

"No, you don't."

"I would have made something out of it, mark my words, Carla."

"I'm making a *video*. Let's try to keep that in mind."

"Tell that to *him*," Dietra said, her red curls moving Fletcher-ward. But when Carla got up the nerve to slide a glance over her shoulder, he had just turned away. Dietra concocted so much unnecessary, unhelpful intrigue!

When the limo arrived Fletcher directed Carla into it with the sheer force of his eyes. The warning behind them told her more clearly than words that, despite her restrained behavior, he was far from believing her as reasonable as she had promised to be. Pretending meekness, she bent her head and got into the car.

Fletcher had not yet settled down; the peculiar tension that had gripped him upon "rescuing" her remained, rendering him almost jumpy and certainly disapproving. She felt a sudden wash of regret for adding to his burden of worry. The carefree aspects of the last several hours had been unusual for him; the demands of his work had not abated. "I'm sorry, Fletcher," she said in a quiet voice. "I appreicate your not wanting me to fall on my head."

Frowning, he met her eyes as if he needed to check her sincerity. Then his expression softened to one of amusement. He replied, almost to himself, "You're a fearless little thing, aren't you?"

"Not *so* little."

His eyes swept over her and the prickles across her neck became waves of heat. He replied enigmatically, "I guess you're a good size."

It was the kind of remark for which Carla knew no possible reply. She puzzled it out in silence. Fletcher grinned and the rest of the ride was easy.

Chapter Four

The rest of the evening was not, although Fletcher proved more sympathetic than he at first threatened and dropped Carla off at her own studio to freshen up and change. The limo returned for her in an hour, a favor for which her flagging body was grateful; even the few blocks up to the Parkside would have killed her. With a shower and presentable suit of clothes, she felt just barely able to face a press conference.

One of the Parkside's many private rooms had been set up with rows of velvet-cushioned chairs and a table with microphones at one end. A fervent-eyed girl at the door presented Carla with a press kit about Mercy Riley and some organization called MAY or, as Carla read from the coversheet, Musicians Alliance for Youth. She realized she had been closely observing *how* Fletcher worked, without noticing *what* he got done. Mercy's national tour would not kick off for another couple of weeks; this Radio City concert was a benefit, not an opening night. The press conference was being held to plug something *other* than Mercy Riley.

None of the principles had shown up yet, just journalists sipping juice and coffee from a side table and MAY workers. Carla slipped off to a corner and tried to acquire a working knowledge of this MAY business. The literature called it a nonpolitical organization of people in the recording and performance industry that supported a broad range of local youth-related projects from drug-rehabilitation centers to musical scholarships. Its proposed philosophy was to "present a positive alternative to the commonly held image that popular and rock music promotes an antisocial, self-destructive lifestyle." Among the founders was listed "Fletcher Arendt, artist manager."

Carla's thoughts arrowed back to the girl with whom Fletcher had supposedly been involved. Dietra claimed she had been wild, the stereotypical young hellion, and she had died in a senseless accident. Had this been the genesis of his commitment to MAY's goals? Carla was touched. She liked to think that blind ambition might not be the first, last and only motive for a man as aggressive as Fletcher Arendt. Then again, ambition *had* to play a big part.

Feeling herself jostled, Carla looked up and discovered the room had filled. Journalists were claiming their seats, two camera crews—one from a local TV station and one from Telemusic—were running last-minute checks. Carla hurriedly set up her own tripod, grateful for the even lighting of the room, but disappointed that she would be stuck in one position by the crowd. She saw Fletcher emerge from a side door, holding the close attention of several reporters, who leaned to catch his words. Carla found herself leaning as well—he looked sensational. The olive-green of his summer suit brought extra gold to his skin and sunny hair. The afternoon's exertion hadn't left him worn out at all, but rather charged with energy. Carla bent grimly to her camera.

Mercy breezed in to an explosion of electronic flashes. She looked gay and effervescent, as well she should, Carla thought, having spent all afternoon lazing in a hotel room. Then she remembered Fletcher's talk of back-to-back interviews and gave the singer due credit. Her white denim western-style skirt and top caught the light brilliantly and her rich chestnut hair flipped attractively whenever she tossed her head. She had movie potential, Carla realized. If she screen-tested well...All the other ingredients of celebrity were there—sex-appeal, beauty, ease before the camera, a bright, mercurial personality. If Fletcher found showcase roles for her, he was going to have a full-blown international star on his hands. He was deft and determined; he'd do it.

Several speakers from MAY took the microphone, then Mercy chattered charmingly about the good work of the organization, told some jokes about her own wild reputation, which drew chuckles from the audience. Carla hadn't read a popular magazine in so long she didn't understand the references. Fletcher's presence in her viewfinder took all her attention. Any tape made here would be good for only a few seconds in the final documentary, since she was frozen into this boring long shot, but Fletcher's expression burned across the distance—grave, intense and slightly melancholy.

The conference broke up after a question-and-answer period that focused more on Mercy Riley than MAY, but no one seemed to mind. The benefit concert had been sold out and any publicity was now simply a bonus.

When Carla saw Fletcher take Mercy's elbow and usher her out through the press of reporters who vied for one last word, she quickly packed up her rig. Common sense told her she'd never push her way into whatever private exit had swallowed them. She'd have to find her way to Mercy's suite and hope to meet up with Fletcher there.

Upstairs, Annette let her in, phone bolted to her ear as always. A maid scurried around removing the traces of the afternoon's company—empty bottles, plates of half-eaten food, magazines flung open across the floor and furniture, hairbrushes, heaps of clothing. It evidently took a lot of turmoil to produce Mercy Riley, singing star.

"Looks like a Nebraska twister hit, doesn't it?" Annette remarked dryly, hanging up the phone.

"Is this normal?"

"Well, she had a small fit this afternoon, did a little pitching practice with the ashtrays. So yes, it's normal. Sit down, you look beat."

"To a pulp," Carla agreed, sinking gratefully back against a couch cushion. "Your Mr. Arendt sets quite a pace."

"Getting any good footage? Oh, here, have a sandwich— that fellow from *Down Home* magazine didn't last long enough to eat any."

"Thanks." Carla chose from a plate of elegantly arranged triangles and fresh vegetable garniture. Until the food touched her tongue she had thought herself too tired to eat. "I'm getting some lively stuff, but it's low quality technically. I'm going to have to balance all the clips I've done on the run with some pieces that are well lit and well recorded. Otherwise I'm going to have an entire documentary that looks like it was taped from the back of a moving stagecoach. Does Fletcher ever sit down?"

Annette fell into a serious pose, tapping her chin with a pencil. "Well...there was that one time in Baton Rouge..."

Carla groaned.

"I'm only kidding. Yeah, he has his stationary moments, though his brain is always whizzing around like a fly inside a screen...argh! What a comparison!"

"I'm sure he'd appreciate it."

"He would," she agreed firmly.

"Annette, why did he decide to let me do this video?"

The brunette inquired carefully, "What did he tell you?"

"That he thought it'd be a good learning experience for Mercy, since she wants to go into films."

"That's all he told *me*. Honest! Not that he'll get far with having sensible reasons...."

"What do you mean?"

"Mercy's determined to be a movie star, but she's not the slightest bit interested in how movies get made. She expects to appear on screen by magic or something. I've tried to throw a few basics her way, Lord knows, but...Still, can't blame Fletcher for trying. He's always felt you should know your craft from the stuffing out."

Of course you should, Carla agreed, stifling a feeling of impatience with Mercy. A frightening thought occurred to her. "Does he know movies as well as he knows music?" He *had* been at that movie production company party...

"No, that's my department. I mean it's *becoming* my department. I majored in film and English in college and was always hoping for a way to work in one or the other. This is heaven-sent, even though everything's strange to me right now. In fact..."

Whatever she had been about to say was lost in the peals of laughter Mercy Riley produced as she tumbled through the door. She was clinging desperately to Fletcher's steadying arm and clutching her stomach. "Oh, Fletch, I thought I'd just *die* the way you handled that awful wart of a man. Imagine the nerve of him! Hello, Nette!"

Carla didn't mind being omitted in the star's greeting—
Fletcher had sent her something that was very nearly a wink
and it made up for Mercy's chill.

"Come on, honey, it's been a long day. Annette will help
you get ready for bed," Fletcher coaxed in the voice one
would use with a child. Carla realized Mercy was slightly
drunk, drunk enough to sway on Fletcher's arm like a sag-
ging door.

"Aw, Fletcher, I thought we were going out tonight to that
jazz club."

"*I'm* going out. *You're* going to bed. Your big show is
tomorrow and I want you to look so beautiful on stage that
you have them jumping out of the fourth mezzanine."

"There are only three mezzanines, Fletcher."

"Just making sure you're paying attention. Now—*bed.*"

"But the club..."

"I'm just doing work tonight, I promise. It's some
unknown trio Dave Tesch told me about. I'm going as a
favor to him."

Mercy sniffed, "Ugh! Dave has the taste of a subway
rat—they're deaf, aren't they? Oops, I lost my balance."
Fletcher scooped her back onto her feet with well-practiced
ease. Mercy continued, irrepressible. "So, you're going all
by your lonesome, honey? A handsome man like you..."

"No, Ms. Copeland is going with me."

This was news to Carla. She held her surprise down to a
lift of the eyebrows.

"Ms. Copeland? Who's Ms. Copeland? Oh." Mercy
examined Carla through unfocused and disappoving eyes.
"Oh yeah. Is she planning on *filming* this unknown,
unsigned, nobody band of Dave's?"

"No, it's part of her research on what managers do,
honey. It gives her background for her documentary."

"Humph" was Mercy's entire comment. She undraped herself from his shoulder and tried to flounce grandly into her room. Annette aimed her through the doorway.

When the two of them were alone Carla studied Fletcher suspiciously. He had very neatly maneuvered things so that her own decision was most definitely made already—of course, someone who was seriously interested in all facets of Fletcher's job would eagerly follow him on a talent hunt, no matter how leaden her bones felt. He had given her such a fine line to walk—on the one hand she had to be full of enthusiasm, on the other she could not seem to be enjoying herself too much or it could be argued that she might be using Fletcher for entrée into a glamorous world. Hadn't he suspected as much at the beginning? The only workable course was to hide every gram of personal feeling—enthusiasm *or* fatigue—and maintain an even, professional bearing, ready for anything her job required, but cool.

"Why, thank you, Fletcher," she said, tingeing her voice with moderate gratitude. "The more I learn, the more dimension I can give to the documentary."

He observed her levelly. "Unless, of course, you're too tired—you've had a rough day."

"Not at all."

"Are you a jazz fan then?"

"In all honesty, no. I've never paid enough attention to jazz to learn its merits."

"Yes, it's a world unto itself," he agreed. "Quite separate from the rock 'n' roll craziness I normally deal with. Or the movie business."

Carla suppressed a shiver and talked herself out of the impression that he had given those last four words an ominous significance. She was just paranoid; she'd have to calm down. She and Fletcher danced around each other like boxers at the beginning of a match, looking for weaknesses.

Hadn't his two previous questions been put to answer exactly the worries she feared he must have—her true motives? They made an awkward pair—two bombs of suspicion primed and set.

With a gesture even Carla could not read as hostile, Fletcher smilingly ushered her through the door. The night had cooled, so they walked to the Forty-fifth Street club and talked lightly of inconsequential things. Fletcher was so easy to talk to when she didn't feel under the microscope. The bright intelligence necessary in his business combined with his humor to produce wry observations on the world. He clearly never felt himself a victim of any situation. He plunged neck-deep into the complex, half-logical flow of life and never lost his footing.

Carla knew that sort of confidence existed, but it had always just eluded her. It wasn't simple arrogance; it balanced recklessness with deep caring. It produced a person who could do drastic things *because* he had a base of instinct and emotion. She didn't know exactly which ingredient she lacked or which was out of balance enough to rock her, but she knew Fletcher had some grip on life that she didn't.

One quality in lavish supply, which didn't necessarily have anything to do with Fletcher's assurance, but couldn't have hurt, was his physical presence. The reaction of every woman who passed reminded Carla that he was a glossy lion of a man, graceful, masculine, vigorous and unusually handsome. The looks of envy that raked her brought a private smile to her lips.

"What are you grinning about?" asked her escort.

She quickly shuffled her face into a less remarkable expression. "Must be the prospect of food. They do serve dinner at this place, don't they?"

"Oh, yes."

"Good, then the evening is on me—a legitimate business expense."

"Well, I'm a great admirer of professionalism," Fletcher proclaimed with the oddest touch of irony. "But there won't be any opportunity tonight. Dave never lets me pay the bill when I go there—he thinks I'm good for the club."

"Are you?"

"Indirectly, maybe. I've pointed a few writers from the music press his way and they've given him good reviews—as they should; he's got an ear for talent, his house bands are always solid."

"I take it Mercy doesn't like jazz."

Fletcher rolled his eyes. "Let's say she's never paid enough attention to it to learn its merits."

After the glitz of Chevrons and the Parkside, Dave's jazz club cuddled Carla in a cocoon of darkness and soft, gentle music. Snug in the theater district, at this time of night it remained half empty, waiting for the after-theater crowds who would want to wind their evening to a slow, easy end.

The maître d' recognized Fletcher and, without fuss, put them in a booth near the stage. Carla sank gratefully into the upholstery and tried to estimate her chances of sleeping unobserved. Pretty slim, she decided—Fletcher looked every bit as alert as he had all day, if a bit more relaxed.

"Is this your last stop of the evening or do you go round the clock?" she inquired.

"Unless you want to film me comatose in bed, this is our last stop."

Carla considered that that might be a nice touch in the documentary, but chose not to say so. "Good, then I'd like to have a drink and let my muscles slump into a puddle on this seat."

"Some wine? A cordial?" A waiter had appeared at Fletcher's elbow.

"Bourbon on ice."

Fletcher chuckled. "A serious drink."

"I'm a serious person."

"Two bourbons then. I'd hate to be the lightweight at the table, I'm so used to being the heavy."

"You could always have a scotch. It took me years to learn to like bourbon, but I'm still working on scotch."

"Do you climb mountains because they're there, Ms. Copeland?"

Carla found the question disturbingly acute; indeed, his penetrating gaze made it so. "Do I seem like such a masochist?" He declined to answer. "Well, I have one overriding belief—If you're going to do something, you should master the hardest parts of it, not just the fun parts— whether you're drinking or making films. Then you have true *freedom* to do your work. I don't think that's masochistic."

"But why do you do what you do? Filmmaking, for instance."

Carla blinked. She hadn't been asked this question in *years,* not since starting film school. At that time she had been filled with earnest theories of how video was the most powerful way to communicate with people raised on movies and television. All her tidy explanations had eventually drifted into the background of her mind, overpowered by the realities of making her way in the world.

So she evaded the question. "I thought *I* was supposed to be uncovering *your* motives, Mr. Arendt. Telemusic's sub- scribers couldn't care less what *I* think. They want to know what *you* think about your work."

"But they'll *get* both, won't they?"

"Touché. I *am* trying to be objective, though, I promise you."

"I believe you, Carla." He smiled and settled deeply into his seat, his hand around the newly arrived bourbon. "But the amateur psychologist in me suggests that maybe you feel safe on your side of the camera and safe doing documentaries."

She was saved from having to respond to this sharp insight by the start of the set. Fletcher's candid eyes were drawn from her to the trio on stage. Bourbon and the supple, lazy jazz lulled her into a state of strangely blurred awareness. The tension of the last several days dissolved; her misused muscles relaxed and for once she stopped planning camera angles. Fletcher was a mysterious, magnetic essence beside her. His deep green suit made him seem one with the subtle darkness, his fair skin and gold hair glowed lucently. He tipped his head down in concentration and Carla saw that his eyes, dipped in shadow, were closed. She closed hers as well, letting the hypnotic notes become her focus. Spellbound by the music's sinuous course, she barely felt the weight of Fletcher's arm press into the top of the cushion behind her neck. It would have been so easy to lean back against him and sink into the deep well of peace he made.

She did not, and the applause at the end of the set brought her groggily to her senses. Fletcher urged her up, some project afire in his eyes. She stumbled after him, diving unimpeded once again into the privileged backstage of the music world. Only his firm grip on her hand kept her moving.

The musicians had collapsed in a little lounge and were swabbing their sweaty faces with towels, discussing the set and accepting the congratulations of friends. Fletcher knocked lightly upon the doorframe. Even in his rather formal suit, he looked comfortable amid the sloppier performers. He fit in wherever he decided to fit. Keeping hold of her hand, he introduced himself and Carla to the trio. The leader rose eagerly, then hung back a bit, trying not to look *too* eager. Carla recognized the symptoms.

"You're very talented," Fletcher said simply. A smile skittered over the face of the little sax player. "Do you have a manager?"

"No," said the pianist. "We make our arrangements ourselves...."

"Get a manager," Fletcher said. "I'll set up an audition for you with Sound Records, if you like. When they start talking about contracts, and they may, you'd better have a manager and/or a very sharp music lawyer."

Three mouths hung open at various levels of disbelief. "What's your cut in this?" they demanded.

Fletcher frowned severely. "*Never* look a gift horse in the mouth, fellows. Now give me a phone number where you can be reached."

In a few minutes this information had been jotted down in Fletcher's ever-present notebook, hands shaken and an escape made. Carla found her hand still tucked into Fletcher's. At first he looked completely unconcerned about the joyous havoc he had just created, then she noted that a magical sparkle lurked in his deep-set eyes.

"I don't get it."

Fletcher waited for her to go on.

"You think they're likely to get a solid recording contract with Sound, but you didn't offer to manage them yourself?"

"I have my hands full right now with Mercy and Billy."

"So...?"

"You're the one uncovering my motives, remember?"

She examined his cheerful face with renewed fervor. "You really get a thrill from helping struggling musicians, don't you?"

"It reminds me...of how people start off—their hopes, their innocence. You can lose sight of it when you get into the 'Mount Olympus' stage of the game.... And, look—here's a cab with your name on it.'' He released her hand in order to flag down the taxi and open its door. When she had climbed inside he leaned through the open window and said, ''Back to mountain-climbing tomorrow, right? I start early.''

''I know,'' she groaned.

''And one more thing...''

''Yes?''

''I still owe you dinner.''

The huge breakfast Carla gulped down the next morning made some amends for her missed dinner, but she would have to be more careful of her health if she expected to match Fletcher's pace for very long.

On arrival at his office she noted gratefully that the companionability of last night had survived into the daytime. His cooperation, and Annette's, knew no bounds. Both endured the setup of lights and sound equipment that would ensure at least a *few* well-taped sequences. Carla began to feel she might get a viable documentary out of this after all.

Most of Fletcher's last-minute, pre-Radio City work proceeded from his desk, so Carla taped busily all day. The surprised people who came to see him were instructed to step carefully over the cables and to ignore the camera. Most succeeded because Fletcher demanded close attention; they soon forgot their surroundings in trying to answer his questions.

During lunch, which she, Fletcher and Annette scraped from deli containers in his office, Carla brought up the proposition that had been on her mind.

''I'd really like to do a sequence where you define your approach to your work, Fletcher. A mini-interview, though

I won't be asking you questions—you'll say whatever you feel is important to get across.''

Annette chuckled over a forkful of potato salad. ''Ah, Fletcher Arendt discourses on the meaning of life.''

Fletcher's eyes twinkled, ''Or at least rock 'n' roll—unless they're the same thing.'' Then he frowned and concentrated with all the seriousness Carla could have wished for. ''That's a big order. You'll have to give me a little time to work on it.''

''Whenever,'' Carla agreed. ''Just tell me when and if you're ready.''

They continued through the afternoon and then, when the New York City sun began to slant sharply through the blinds, he told her he was ready. He had worn a thoughtful expression during the brief interludes when no one sat across from him talking, or when the phones lay silent. Evidently he had been thinking of Carla's request.

She lit him carefully so that the slatted light seemed to make his face move in and out of mystery. Smoke from his latest neglected cigarette furled through the air like the presence of half-revealed thoughts and memories. Softly, so as not to break his mood, she told him she had started the camera. He remained in meditative silence for a few more moments, then, without any uncertainty, he began.

''When I was a criminal justice lawyer I thought that I was seeing the very worst society had to offer—bare-faced crime at its ugliest, murderers, thieves, con artists. Day in and day out I waded through it, amazed at the beauty of the rest of the world and how separate it seemed. I'd come home after a session at night court and fall asleep dreaming to some glorious piece of music and it would serve to remind me that there was a better world somewhere.

''It was a really romantic notion. I had friends who were artists and they had to live in the regular world just as I did.

It was when they let their art take them over that you saw proof of the light they kept inside. But what the world did to them came so close to killing that light. Sometimes it literally killed the artist. Because, of course, the world works the same everywhere—out on the street, backstage, in corporate offices. There's ugliness everywhere making a rough living out of the innocent and the weak.

"I knew I was neither innocent nor weak and so I decided that, rather than prosecute the scum and try to keep them away from society, I would go at it from the opposite side. I would protect the victims, specifically the artists. And so I became a manager—kind of the hard shell around the pearl.

"The great irony of it is that I have to beat the rats at their own game. In order to outmaneuver them, I have to be even more ruthless and cold-blooded than they are."

He looked up then, straight into Carla's lens, his eyes dark with the depth of his thoughts. "And I *am*. No one will remember Fletcher Arendt because he was a sweetheart, but they'll remember his artists because they survived long enough to make their art."

He fell silent. It took Carla several moments to snap out of the rapt attention he had commanded and shut off the camera.

"Was that what you wanted?" he asked quietly.

"Yes."

His phone rang then and he reached quickly to answer it, stepping back into stride with no apparent effort. Carla struggled to recover. The speech had been just what she had wanted but hadn't had the nerve to hope for. She could have made the same points in a narrative voice-over, but his face, his measured voice summing up the essence of the man made a more powerful statement than any she could have concocted secondhand. How many filmmakers were blessed with such cooperative, capable subjects?

Her private session with Fletcher ended when he announced that he must collect Mercy for the concert. Since it was still hours until concert time, Carla correctly assumed he needed to do a bit of nerve-calming beforehand.

The population of the Parkside suite had greatly increased. In addition to Annette, three other young women and half a dozen men sprawled on the furniture amid the remains of takeout Chinese food. One bearded fellow strummed lazily at a guitar and two of the women hummed a line of harmony. Carla surmised that they were Mercy's backup band. Mercy herself was not to be seen.

"She's panicking in her room," one of the girls whispered. Fletcher promptly disappeared in that direction and did not return until concert time. With her main subject out of reach and a shyness about intruding on whatever rituals the band might need to psyche themselves for the stage, Carla kept a low profile, nibbling on spareribs and checking her rig.

When Fletcher emerged later, to announce that it was time to leave, Mercy accompanied him, as clear-eyed and self-possessed as Carla had ever seen her. Dressed in her stage costume, she also looked gorgeous and illuminated by eagerness. The excitement infected everyone, from the bland Annette to Carla herself.

She needed all her adrenaline that night. She attacked Radio City Music Hall like an armed mole, following Fletcher through its complicated innards—from the production office to the dressing rooms; from the underground hydraulic stage lifts to the stage manager's booth in the wings; from the projection rooms high above the third mezzanine to the ticket office. Part of her incentive for sticking to Fletcher like a burr was the suspicion that she'd get hopelessly lost on her own. The backstage facilities were connected by long, beige corridors that zigged and zagged dizzyingly up through layer upon layer of offices, rehearsal studios, costume departments, lighting coves, staff elevators, screening rooms and an infinite number of nooks and crannies.

Midway through the concert Carla found herself pausing with Fletcher at the rear of the auditorium in the booths that housed the huge spotlights. The view through the spotlight bays was arresting—far below the audience sat hushed in the gracefully curving rows of red velvet seats, their faces turned raptly toward the stage. Three soft, celestial beams of white light arrowed through the smoky air and overlapped in a clover about Mercy's feet. She was dressed in pure white, the fringe of her suede dress swept in luminous ripples as she sang something slow and melancholy. Her strong, pure alto made the hall ring like the dome of a bell.

Mesmerized, Carla shifted the camera away from her face and propped herself against a wall to listen. The voices of the spotlight operators as they talked to the stage manager through their headsets faded to nothing. She forgot to notice how the heat from the big lamps made her sweat. The tune registered as one that had been played constantly on the radio last winter—Mercy's big hit "Bitterly True." She had introduced it solemnly: "I wrote this song for a friend of mine who was never able to hear it."

For the first time Carla paid attention to the lyrics:

How could I have stopped you?
But why did I let you go?
More than my soul died with you.
Life is a teacher
And love is the lesson
Belatedly, bitterly true...

Directed by the poignant regret in the song, Carla's eyes strayed to a dim white shape at the other end of the booth. Fletcher leaned one arm against the spotlight bay, his forehead pressed against it and his eyes forlorn. Did the song so affect him? Did he still think in misery of the girl who had died?

Carla felt a sudden, acute wretchedness. Mercy, for all her childishness, had shared with Fletcher years of hopes and dreams and memories. They were bound together, if not by romance, then by these. What had Carla shared with him? She was nothing to him but a liability. She hadn't wanted to discover warm feelings for this man, but there they lay, as messy and unavoidable as a flooded basement.

The song ended and the source of her soggy feelings roused himself with a catlike shake. Quicker than she could collect her wits, he dashed off, called to yet another task. This time Carla lost him. It annoyed her, considering her vow to keep up with him all evening. She sat in the band's dressing room next door to Mercy's and watched the end of the concert on the in-house video monitor. Mercy came out for three encores, curtsying prettily and thanking everyone for the support they had given to MAY.

A few minutes later the band itself clattered into the dressing room, exhausted but giddy with the success of their performance. Carla assured them that they had been as sensational as they thought they had been. How like actors they were, needing this reassurance and getting so high on their work.

Mercy popped her head in the doorway and the mutual congratulations intensified. Carla saw Fletcher lounging across the hall, letting his star enjoy the exhilaration of her band. He had a radiant look of satisfaction on his face, in contrast to the melancholy she had last seen. Was he such a creature of moods? So few men showed their feelings at all—it was hard for her to fit him in with his cold, cutthroat busines.

Mercy waved a light good-bye and headed for her own dressing room. Before joining her, Fletcher leaned in the doorway and said in his deep, tranquil voice, "It was a really good show—so quit worrying about the tour, okay? And I'll see you at the party."

His few words created a quiet but seemingly more intense pleasure than all of Mercy's flutter. The lead guitarist let out a low whistle. "You heard the boss—we deserve a party!" They quickly began to dive for fresh clothes and towels; Carla thought it appropriate to leave.

She wheeled her trolley into the hall, hoping Fletcher might pop out of Mercy's dressing room and spend a minute or two with her. She could use a little information on their immediate plans; she could also use a dose of his warming company. She had to stop short of Mercy's door in order to restrap some flapping cables and, as she worked, her ears picked up the high-pitched whine of the star at her most annoying.

"I hope you're not planning to float off and leave me alone at the party tonight with all those bores, Fletcher."

His words, so soothing as to be nearly inaudible, drew Carla's unwilling attention. "Of course not, honey. You know I stand by you in all this PR work."

"Humph," Mercy snorted. "Seems like you've been plenty glad to abandon me lately and skip off with that camera-toting female. She's getting a nice ride out of this documentary hogwash—parties, jazz clubs, access to the private lives of me and my band. You know, I'm surprised at you, Fletcher; you're the last one I'd ever thought could get sucked in by such an obvious little scheme."

Carla's back had stiffened like a board and Fletcher's reply failed to relax her. His voice was firm, but hardly as chastising as Carla would have liked. "It's pretty late in the game to lose faith in me, Mercy, and I don't think you've ever had any cause to complain, have you?" She mumbled something indistinct. "I think my reasons for cooperating with this documentary are unarguably in your interests—you *do* still want this film career, I presume. If not, *tell me*— we're going out on a limb for it, calling in favors, making riskier deals than I usually like, cultivating people I'd never have anything to do with otherwise. Hmm? Am I still working for you?"

"Oh, Fletcher..." Mercy grumbled reluctantly. "Of course. I just...I'm just a little cranky, I guess."

A sudden shadow in the doorway caused Carla to scuttle twenty feet farther back down the hall so no one would catch her eavesdropping. She knelt by her trolley, trying to control the wave of nausea that had flooded her. What in *particular* had she just heard that should make her feel so queasy? Nothing, strictly speaking—just a lot of vague talk. She had wanted Fletcher to squelch his star's accusations by some bold statement along the lines of "Ms. Copeland's talents as a filmmaker are above reproach. Even if I saw no direct benefit to your film career, I would want her here working on this documentary." That would have been the fairy-tale answer. The real answer had to do with compromise and Fletcher's inscrutable master plan. As to that, Carla, at least, knew he was as shrewd and capable a planner as anyone she had ever met.

She could very well be one of the people he'd never have anything to do with were it not for Mercy's film hopes. That knowledge, and her constant fear that her mother's fame hung ready to drop on her like a sticky net, unnerved her into a more demoralizing worry—what if he *did* know who she was? She had been so anxious to believe in his change of heart—his story of wanting her to teach Mercy about the film business—perhaps she had overlooked the better reason....

"Fellini!" The familiar voice jerked her head up. Fletcher strode down the hall toward her, wearing his immovably pleasant expression, as if he had not just had a row with his client. "Can you park that eighteen-wheeler of yours someplace? The promoter's throwing a party at the Parkside for MAY and two hundred of his own closest personal friends. You could count it as more research for your flick."

"No, I don't think so," she began slowly. For lack of a reasonable excuse, she let Fletcher raise her to her feet with one hand while she thought. She didn't know if he kept hold of her an extra second or if her sense of time simply stretched it into a miserable eternity.

"No? Whoever heard of a pretty young woman refusing a party?" His smile blossomed, warm and coaxing.

Carla chased after words that would make it sound as if she had actually based her refusal on rational thought. "Really, there's only so much information I can get from a promoter's party. I think I should go home and start making sense of the actual tape I've got. We're piling up a good deal of it, you know."

He frowned, perplexed. "Maybe you deserve a little break then—these parties *can* be fun."

She drew herself up stiffly. "I'm not in this for *fun*."

He frowned even harder, his dark brows stormy over light-shot eyes. "I see, of course not."

They stood looking at each other, Carla uncomfortable, Fletcher enigmatic, until he finally said in a brisk, emotionless tone, "Then I'll see you tomorrow morning for Mercy's costume fitting. Annette will give you the address."

She gulped, nodded and walked collectedly toward the elevator, dragging her rig and feeling his eyes stab her back like diamond drill bits.

Chapter Five

Adrian Macklin, the designer, was a large, round woman, long past her glamorous youth as a model, but still striking. She opened the door of the penthouse overlooking Gramercy Park, raised her thin, drawn-on blond eyebrows at Carla's camera and then ushered her in with an expression of apology. What she was sorry for became apparent as soon as Carla left the pink-and-white marble foyer and entered the pink-and-white-draped salon.

Mercy paced the floor like a caged cat, taking random kicks at flamingo-colored throw pillows and bolts of expensive-looking fabric. She showed the effects of the concert and the party on her strained face and in her temper. Carla judged it a wise time to hide the camera behind a chair.

"Where is he?" the star demanded in a raspy voice quite alien to her usual mellow croon. Carla noticed that three cigarettes smeared with Mercy's shade of lipstick burned in various porcelain ashtrays. A haze of blue-gray smoke hung in the air. This couldn't be the healthiest habit for a singer, Carla thought privately.

"He's late!" Mercy snarled.

Adrian drawled in a deep voice almost as soothing as Fletcher's, "No, *you're* late. He was here an hour ago and you weren't. I told you that he left again to run an errand."

Mercy glared poisonously; she didn't like being corrected. "What am I supposed to do—*guess* what he has in mind for all these damn clothes?" She glared now specifically at Carla. "Or maybe you're supposed to videotape me so he can watch when he gets around to it."

Without Fletcher's mollifying influence, Carla's sarcasm demanded free rein. "Actually, this video is about *him;* anyone else is purely added color."

Mercy froze, appalled. Carla couldn't believe the words that had boiled from her own mouth, though there had been several occasions when she dearly would have liked to say some such thing to this temperamental brat.

All the same, she had just carelessly upset one of Fletcher's clients. He'd *love* that.

Before the singer could retaliate, the doorbell chimed. Stifling a large grin, Adrian leaped to answer it. Greetings sounded in a husky voice and Fletcher entered the room. His appearance threw Mercy's tantrum into shadow. Each time Carla saw him she was newly struck by the man's presence; he filled the room with a vitality, a sense of energy and vibrant possibility that dispelled paler concerns as the sun burned off fog.

This morning, appropriately, he wore a linen suit the parched color of an African savanna and a white shirt open at the base of his golden throat. He didn't seem afflicted by any of Mercy's tired peevishness. He wouldn't. Carla stood utterly still, fighting off the feeling of attraction, remembering her very precarious position in his world.

Mercy, perhaps inured by familiarity to such beauty, stormed across the dainty room like a thunderhead, ready to let loose her torrent of anger. She got as far as opening her mouth. Then Fletcher leaned down, kissed her cheek and said, quietly but clearly, "Shut up and let's get to work."

It cured Mercy instantly. Fletcher lifted his blond head, caught Carla's eye and winked. "I hope you're all famished," he said expansively. "I brought breakfast." He gestured, and a teenaged boy in a white coat that said "Byron's Gourmet Deli" carted in a large picnic basket and began to set out linen and silverware on a long coffee table. Adrian hummed with pleasure and made herself comfortable on a pink taffeta chair.

Out of the basket came cold, dewy fruit, golden croissants, several wedges of cheese and a ceramic crock of butter. With a great flourish, the boy then produced a bottle of cold duck and four long-stemmed glasses.

Adrian fell upon the feast with no self-consciousness. Mercy deigned to accept a glass of wine and resumed her agitated pacing. She continued to mumble complaints to which Fletcher listened with a tolerant, if only half-attending, ear. He placed a rosy nectarine, a croissant and a slice of hard orange cheddar on a plate and brought it to Carla. "Got to keep your strength up, Fellini. Although this is *not* the meal I owe you."

Carla wondered if she looked particularly wretched and weak today or if he was just making conversation. As she took the plate she saw her own small, pale hand against his strong one of toasted gold and sighed. If it wasn't enough that she had to prove herself a skilled filmmaker, she also had to cope with people's fears that she'd break.

Mercy's acid drawl interrupted them. "Anytime you can drag yourself away, Fletcher."

Fletcher refused to be provoked. He continued to gaze speculatively at Carla from a distance so slight she could see the very beginnings of a golden beard blurring his cheeks. She liked the scruff; it softened the rigorous lines of his jaw as nothing could blunt the rigor of his personality.

As he continued to stare in his intense way, that rigorousness began to make her uncomfortable. Carla felt she was being examined through a microscope. To break the moment, she asked very quietly, "Will I be able to tape anything this morning?"

"We'll see," he said unhopefully, sliding a glance toward Mercy.

Although trying on costumes distracted her for short periods of time, Mercy's temper did not improve enough to admit the camera. Adrian had just finished the line for the tour; nothing remained to be done but making a few final, meticulous adjustments of fit and ornament. Fletcher examined everything with a keen eye and proved to have a sensitivity to nuance that would have done the designer herself credit. Mercy twirled and fussed. Adrian pinned and draped and explained how each outfit could be used for the most dramatic effect. Both waited expectantly for Fletcher's comments; he invariably came up with the one overlooked detail, the one item that didn't work as well as it should.

"That belt is too stiff—I think a suede sash would lie more gracefully on Mercy's hips...."

"Wear your hair up with that one, honey, it'll show off that swan's neck of yours...."

"Where'd you get the fabric, Adrian? From a feedstore?"

"Too dark still. Can you have more pearls beaded into the bodice?"

How did a man who could move the wheels of record companies and concert halls come by his intimate knowledge of women's fashion? The skills seemed light years apart and both were demanding enough to take one's full attention. Carla herself could design a lighting scheme for a large production and then, just as easily, sit down and make changes in an actor's makeup, but this flexibility was required by one in her business; she never expected to find it in someone else.

During a break Adrian disappeared into the kitchen to make coffee. Mercy stationed herself so possessively at Fletcher's side that Carla decided to go help Adrian. She followed the designer through long mirrored halls into a huge room of white tile, copper trim and butcher-block counters. Carla had expected an artsy, flamboyant kitchen, not one as functional and well-stocked as a showroom. Adrian, sensing her surprise, explained, "I like to say I'm doing my bit to support all the hard-working designers and inventors out there who are dreaming up new ways to core apples."

Carla laughed, tickled by such a noble philosophy. "I see!"

Adrian laughed with her. "Well, at least I've got a *reason* for my addiction, even if it is silly. What's your excuse?"

"For what?"

"For devoting a day of your artistic life to watching a torch singer primp?"

"I had hoped to get some taping done today."

"Ah yes, Fletcher mentioned your project...."

"What did he say about it...or *how* did he sound when he mentioned it?"

Adrian matched her squint for squint. "Is he giving you a hard time?"

"Oh, no! He's being exceedingly cooperative. But I guess I'm just not sure of *why*. I mean, it's a big intrusion into his life."

"Well, my dear, you can be sure he's got his reasons. Here, grind these beans." She stretched for a box of coffee filters on a top shelf, grunting with the effort. "You can tell that *men* design kitchens—no woman of average height can reach her own shelves. Anyway, why do you *think* he's cooperating?"

Carla avoided answering while she ran the grinder. Then, as she swept the stray grounds from the glossy, tiled counter into a wastebasket, she replied dubiously, "Well, he said something about having me around to teach Mercy film-making. But Mercy is about as interested in filmmaking as she is in...in..."

"In anything other than herself?" Adrian suggested dryly.

"I wasn't going to say that."

"No, but it probably isn't too far wrong. Hell, who knows what goes through the dark, circuitous labyrinth of the mind of a man like Fletcher Arendt? I've been working with him for two of Mercy's tours now and he's still a mystery man." Her round eyes stared intently at Carla. "But did you ever consider the obvious?"

"*What* obvious?" asked Carla, alarmed.

"He might be interested in you—I mean *romantically.*"

This unnerving possibility was given jarring emphasis by the appearance of the man under discussion.

"I thought for a minute there that I smelled coffee, but none showed up, so I decided I'd better come after it. I see grounds, I see hot water..." He raised his eyebrows suggestively.

"Carla was about to put them together."

"Good, because Mercy's calling for you, Adrian. She says you pinned the dress to her and now she can't get out."

"All right. That means I have to trust you to help Carla, Lord preserve us. Now remember, you bossy thing, *she's* in charge." And Adrian bustled out.

Fletcher walked up to Carla's elbow, his hands clasped demurely behind his back and a very playful smile sparkling through the amber fuzz of beard. "I am yours to command."

Carla doubted it; he was probably as expert in the kitchen as he was everywhere else. He was also standing too close to her, casting a warm glow on her back and shoulders as she leaned determinedly onto the counter. Her feelings had been unsettled enough before he came; now they would have *no* chance to sort themselves out.

"Try to find some cups," she ordered.

"Yes, ma'am." He then reached into the cabinet directly over her head. She sternly fought down an urge to bolt—it was as strong as the one to lean back and rest against his broad, solid chest and have his beautiful, tanned arms close around her. Instead she twisted about, hoping she would seem to be casually slipping off to the side in search of...spoons or something. She fetched up against Fletcher's free arm, which he had just inconveniently braced against the countertop. She now stood disconcertingly face to face or, at least, face to chin with him.

"My, you're a skittish little thing," he growled softly. The other hand brought down a cup and then set itself on the counter at her other hip.

"Déjà vu," she remarked, trying grimly to be flip.

"Are you referring to the time you tried to fly off the amp crate?"

"Yes, the time I conceded that you might have had a reason for...to..."

"I was trying to save you, I believe."

"So you said."

"Maybe I'm still trying to save you," he suggested.

Surprised out of her self-consciousness, she demanded, "From what?"

"From getting too wrapped up in your illusions, Fellini. You're always looking at me through that darned viewfinder. Do you ever see me as a man?"

She would have pointed out that she had no choice at the moment, considering how he had pinned her against the counter with his arms and hips. She *would* have said this, but his words had brushed her lips like a kiss and, as soon as their sound had disappeared into the curls behind her ears, he did kiss her. He was tender, teasing; he allowed his mouth to touch hers for no longer than it took her to feel it. He played and tickled and coaxed the resistance from her with his warmth and breath. Prepared for a hard assault, she barely had the presence of mind to push his mouth away with hot fingertips.

"Please don't do this," she tried to request in a reasonable voice. It came out a whisper.

But Fletcher's half-lidded eyes showed no sympathy. His hands seared her back, pulling her shoulders toward him, his fingers tangled in her hair, his teeth nipped the edges of her lips until she softened them for fear of being bitten. This was a mistake; his molten taste and his strength intoxicated her. She felt he couldn't kiss her deeply enough or hold her too hard. She brought one hand up to stroke his jaw's new roughness, the other skimmed the velvet skin of his neck. Her muscles dissolved in the forge of his incandescent body, his fiery, peremptory power. She had tried to capture passion before—on film, with lights and angles and words. She had never allowed herself to feel it until now. Her strength burned away. When he dragged her head back and broke their kiss with a ragged sigh she could not take her own weight; for an instant she could not breathe for herself.

"I knew I could find you again," he remarked in a murmur. She regained her senses enough to be puzzled. His hot blue eyes held her in alarmingly sharp focus. "I knew you weren't that cool, untouchable hired hand we've had around here these last couple of days."

She stiffened uncontrollably, her limbs suddenly finding their resistance. Anger clenched her jaw so tight she could barely speak. "So that's what this is all about—another way to make me shut up, or to shake me, or get whatever reaction you've decided on, right?"

He shook his head in what seemed disgust. "I should never have let you use your mouth to talk."

"That's insulting and patronizing!" she spat, wrenching violently and getting nowhere. The feel of his thighs hard on hers and his iron arms had become oppressive.

"I know—I should shut up, too. We both do a lot better on a different level entirely."

"And is it your purpose in life to keep dragging me down to that level?"

"You know, you distort every word I say, every move and every look. We're not going to end up with a documentary at all, no matter how you playact that you're an objective videojournalist."

"Then you'd better fire me and save yourself from all the vicious distortions I'm bound to spread about you."

"Oh, no," he declared, a funny smile edging into the corners of his fire-lashed eyes. "I'm not letting you off that easily. You stop now and I'll never have justice, will I? You'll go off in a righteous huff with all these ideas that I'm an arrogant, tyrannical, conceited—come on, help me with the list...."

"You're doing all right," she countered.

"Masochistic I'm not. Anyway, I'm not going to let you take the easy way out just because you're afraid."

"Afraid of what?" she demanded indignantly.

His smile was sly and honey-sweet. "Among other things—of me."

"Ha!" she tried to say. His unrelenting grasp denied her enough breath to make it truly explosive. "Fear of being *manhandled* is not the same as fear of *you*."

"How about fear of your feelings?"

"And you, of course, know exactly what they are?"

"I've picked up a few clues." His blatant grin infuriated her.

"Speaking of 'picking up'—why don't you put me down?"

"All right," he said equably, but instead of immediately complying, he pulled her away from the counter and drew his hands slowly down from her shoulders, into the scoop of her waist and over the curve of her buttocks. She remained unresponsively rigid.

As he finally released her, she asked bitingly. "Trying to prove something?"

"No, just giving you one last little bit to think about."

"Don't count on it."

He tipped his head in a mocking salute and started to turn away.

"Fletcher!" He gave her his perfect attention. "What has this been all about? What is it you *want* from me?"

"What do you have to give?" Without waiting for an answer, he left her to the bright, slick surfaces of the empty kitchen.

By the time Carla had settled her anger down to a low simmer, Adrian poked a tentative face around the frame of the door.

"Hmmm...nothing broken, I see."

Carla looked up warily, unsure what reception her own admittedly suspicious behavior might merit. She had been sulking in the kitchen of a total stranger for...how long? The designer came fully into the room, knuckles planted on one hip and a bemused expression on her placid face.

"I'm sorry," Carla mumbled uncomfortably. "I haven't even made the coffee yet. I got a bit...lost in thought."

"Well, no loss. There's no one to drink it but us."

"Why not?"

"Fletcher dragged Mercy off by the scruff of the neck a few minutes ago. I'm left with four pounds of fancy cheese and a dozen croissants. Too bad Mercy made such short work of the cold duck...."

"Why did they leave?"

Adrian's skinny brows pushed shallow lines into her dry forehead. "I hoped maybe you could throw a little light on that." Carla felt a hot flush sear her cheeks. "Guess not. Far as I can tell, Mercy just got a bit too sassy even for Fletcher—and he's hauling her off to solitary confinement at her hotel. Boy, did *his* face look like a thundercloud."

Carla had turned around to keep her affliction from Adrian's keen eyes and was stacking the saucers.

"Oh, hell, make the coffee anyway, doll. No reason we can't have some food at Fletcher's expense."

The thought appealed to Carla's prickly state of mind. She certainly wouldn't know what to do with herself loose on the street right then and Adrian's down-to-earth humor was soothing.

They settled in the salon, in the midst of Mercy's last temper tantrum—when she had apparently said something too flip for even Fletcher. The gorgeous clothes had been kicked or thrown over the furniture and half an apple lay in the middle of the dusty pink carpet. Adrian tossed out the apple but let the rest lie.

"Won't those outfits wrinkle?"

Adrian dismissed them with a careless gesture. "Nah, they're designed for the abuse they'll get on a tour—this is nothing. Have a croissant."

Carla's thoughts drifted over the rubble and out toward the city streets as she layered butter onto the roll. She became aware of the designer's amused glance. "Ah, to be young and skinny." Adrian sighed.

"Oops, that's a little too much butter even for me."

"There's bound to be a bit of philosophy waiting to be quoted here—something about enjoying the pleasures of life—you know, 'Gather ye rosebuds while ye may.' Oh, well." Adrian shifted and began dumping sugar into her coffee. "Now that I'm an old bat I'm supposed to be full of wisdom and ready to dispense it to all you callow young things, but..."

"You're hardly an old bat."

"I'm not terribly wise either. So here we are—a pair of fools."

Fortuitously the telephone rang. Adrian lumbered to answer it. "Hello?...Hey, my carpet is still smoking from your blazing departure, young man!" She covered the mouthpiece and whispered, "It's Fletcher calling from his car phone."

Carla started to rock her knuckles nervously on the table.

Adrian listened, humming an occasional response. "I see. Yes, I'll tell her.... He says he forgot to tell you that you're supposed to have dinner with him and someone called Bob Rhoades tonight...."

Carla shook her head emphatically.

"She's saying 'no,' Fletcher.... Ah...ah, okay...He says he's not asking you. Rhoades wants to meet Telemusic's documentary maker—this counts as instructions from On High, Fletcher says...." Her attention returned to the phone, she scribbled something on a nearby pad. "Yes, I've got it...oh, nice place! I don't suppose he wants to meet the costume designer, too..., Didn't think so. Well, have the veal *cordon bleu* for me—it's out of this world.... Oh, yes, the costumes will be ready for Her Majesty on Wednesday. Ta.'' Adrian returned, bearing the scrap of paper. "Here— he says to meet him and Rhoades at the China Clipper on East Sixty-fifth Street at seven-thirty tonight. It's terribly posh, too—I've been there all of two times, both on some- one else's expense account.... Why are you growling at that poor plate?''

Carla raised her head, suddenly self-conscious, but no less angry. "He has his nerve.''

"Oh, yeah, no one ever said Fletcher Arendt was weak- willed.''

"But that was *underhanded.* He didn't even ask me face to face.''

"Maybe he really did forget. Maybe he had something more compelling on his mind while he was here.'' If Adrian meant anything in particular by this, she blunted her mean- ing by sliding her eyes away. "Anyway, you get to dress up and have a sensational meal at the mere cost of putting up with one of the most attractive men in North America.''

"Bob Rhoades?''

Adrian blinked, quite at a loss. Then she said tentatively, "You want to tell me exactly what your relationship with Fletcher is?''

"No. But if one more person tells me I lack the normal responses of a healthy human female, I'll jump up and down on their larynx.''

Adrian switched instantly into a light, admonishing man- ner. "Who's been telling you that? Nonsense! A woman is a woman. Men just get nervous when they don't know where they stand and they blame it on her.''

"As if *she's* deficient.''

"Exactly. Poor things. They need to have it spelled out for them—you know, having the woman dress up to please them, having her melt in their arms, with her eyes out of focus and her breath short...."

"Adrian!"

"Oh, am I getting carried away?"

"A bit."

"Well, it's my stock in trade, knowing all this stuff about nonverbal communication—what colors are sensual, how low to cut the neckline...You know it, too, as a filmmaker."

"I make documentaries, not fantasies," Carla corrected, stomping down hard on the memory of Fletcher's criticism.

Adrian looked disappointed. "Oh, too bad. Well, at least you've got the services of someone who does."

Carla laughed. "You mean you intend to dress me for this confounded dinner?"

"Don't you think it'd be fun? *I'd* get a kick out of it. You know, I've been lavishing my creative juice on that prima donna Mercy Riley for two years, sitting here listening to Fletcher critique my work like some professor at fashion school, and never once have I gotten a true emotional reaction from him!" The designer had begun to pace, her round face puckering in a frown of annoyance. "He's so observant, really sensitive. You saw how he noticed everything and knew what effect each costume would create. But nothing ever gets through to him. I suppose it's because he's so used to seeing Mercy as his client, his cause. He may love her, but he's not *in* love with her."

"A man can react without being in love with what he sees."

"So they say. But Fletcher is not your usual construction worker whistling at everything that passes by in a skirt."

Carla accepted this without comment.

Caught up in her own plans, Adrian went on, "I don't know what it takes to get to him, but I'd sure like to do it. My professional pride is involved."

"Adrian, I think you're exaggerating."

The designer stopped and wrinkled her nose in vexation. "You're mean!"

Carla laughed outright and Adrian joined her. The older woman's little piece of melodrama had revealed her fanciful, childlike side and broken down some of Carla's lingering reserve. Adrian reminded her of Dietra, carrying herself away with her own enthusiasms, totally without guilt.

The designer came back to the table and sat down to her tepid coffee. "Humpf. Spoilsport. But I'll have my way, you'll see."

"Oh, yeah?"

"Yep. Tell me, do you *have* a dress suitable for a swank place like the China Clipper?"

Carla thought furiously...and thought some more.

"I figured you wouldn't," Adrian announced smugly. "Are you prepared to spend the rest of the day and the rest of your bank account shopping for one? No, huh? Well, I've got dozens of dresses I made for the hell of it that are rotting in my closets. How about you let me slap something on your back just to make both of us happier?"

Carla sighed.

Chapter Six

Fletcher stared morosely into his double bourbon and realized from the bartender's veiled looks of distress that he had unknowingly shredded four cocktail napkins in the past ten minutes. He fixed one hand firmly in his jacket pocket and clamped the other around his drink. Within seconds he was spinning the glass in noisy circles all over the glossy mahogany bar. What was his problem tonight? He must have some weird disease that caused rapid deterioration of the nervous system; such agitation and black humor were not usual with him.

He didn't usually make huge, clonking mistakes with people either, but he had been far from his normal deft self these past few days. He *knew* how to handle Carla; he knew it was of the utmost importance for her to be treated as the professional she strove to be. And if Bob Rhoades said one word sideways about movies that evening it would be his last utterance on earth. Fletcher had laid down a deadly ulti-

matum—keep the conversation *off* filmmaking or quake
with fear when Mercy's contract came up for renewal.
Rhoades was a tasteless, coarse manipulator, but he would
recognize a serious threat.

The more mystifying question remained: why couldn't
Fletcher leave Carla alone? Why did he keep turning to her
and, unable to shut himself up, say or do the one thing guar-
anteed to ignite her? Of course she had enough grit to fight
back. Mercy crumpled under rough treatment. Billy lost
confidence. Annette refused to be provoked. Carla returned
blow for blow.

But why should she have to? Her sexual attractiveness
didn't explain it. He had never had to attack women to get
them into his arms. Past experience suggested that she, too,
could be talked and coaxed into bed if that's what he
wanted—and that was something like what he wanted, but
not quite—not quite.

Fletcher finished off the bourbon in a gulp, as if the fiery
wash of alcohol could burn the other discomfort out of his
chest. Damn Carla Copeland anyway! He couldn't really
care so much about her; it was just some bizarre conjunc-
tion of planets or the disorienting early summer heat or perhaps a virus that made him so sensitive to her.

He stood up decisively, compelled to do something simple and sensible to restore faith in his sanity—something like
get a table—when he spied the maddening woman herself,
consulting with the maître d'. She was a shimmer of gold,
from the tips of her little feet to the great cloud of wild, red-
gold curls that framed her heart-shaped face. He swore
crossly under his breath. Why wasn't she conventionally
beautiful—he could ignore that—instead of fragile and
bright as a snowflake?

Grimly, he walked up to meet her. Her green eyes were
unreadable. "Good evening, Fletcher," she said.

He knew from her tone of voice that she intended to be cool again, unflappable as if their stormy scenes together had been something easily edited out of one of her videos. In other words, he had a fresh chance to behave as a rational human being. He had a lot of experience; he *ought* to be able to manage it.

"You look lovely tonight," he ventured sincerely. He hoped she would see it as an innocuous nicety.

"Thank you. Has Mr. Rhoades arrived yet?"

"No. Frankly, I don't expect him for quite a while yet. He seems to think that being late is the mark of a VIP."

"Gee, I like him already."

Her humor cheered him; at least she wasn't going to act like a martyr. "Shall we get a table and make ourselves comfortable?"

"Will they mind us taking up the space and not ordering?"

He smiled. "They'd better not—I'm one of their best customers." He signaled to the maître d' and followed Carla as they were escorted to a table that offered a matchless view of the light-studded East River; Fletcher's usual table, in fact, though he did not see the use of mentioning this. Carla slid gracefully into the deeply cushioned armchair and draped her gold wrap over the back. The fine alabaster of her shoulders put the opulent fabric to shame, her hair dimmed its rich gold. Fletcher quickly attended to the quiet waiter who had appeared at his elbow. "Bourbon, Carla?"

"Please."

"Two bourbons then, ice and water. Oh, and that special hors d'oeuvre tray, if Pierre still has the patience to make it."

"He does indeed, Mr. Arendt. Do you still prefer the black caviar to the red?"

"How about it, Carla?" Fletcher inquired. "Do you have a preference?"

"No, black is fine."

When they were alone again Carla's disapproving face bewildered him. "What's the matter? Did you want red?"

She tossed her curls; he had always thought it an affected gesture on the part of women who had pretty hair, but he saw it now as the expression of an emotion she simply refused to let out. "You really *are* a regular, aren't you?"

"It's a good place to bring people you're trying to impress," he said frankly.

"I'm sure. It's just that..."

He leaned forward, interested in what might have caused her scorn. "Just that...what?"

She glowered fiercely. Then she faced him with eyes that threw off golden sparks like an unmanageable fire. "I *hate* all this, you know."

"All this *what*?"

"All this nonsense about fancy restaurants where they give you the best table if you're somebody, and clubs where you get put on the guest list if you're somebody, and parties only somebodies get invited to." She stopped for breath, tensely chewing her peach-tinted lips. He wanted to put out a finger to stop her. He forebore, suspecting that it would get bitten off.

"Tell me," she continued. "Does all this make Mercy's music any better? Or Billy's?"

"No," he replied simply.

"Will it make my video any better?"

"I don't know. You tell me."

"No! In fact, I find all this extracurricular stuff distracting and I resent that people get to see me constantly immersed in the glamour you're surrounded by. It looks as if I'm sponging off it somehow, coming along for the ride."

Fletcher leaned back in his chair and fixed her with a stern, imperative gaze. "Why the hell do you *care* what anybody else thinks?"

She stopped, momentarily perplexed. Then she rallied, but some of her fury was gone. "Well, there's the small matter that my future jobs will come from people who may have formed their opinion of me through my social life, rather than my work."

"You want to be invisible, don't you—behind your work?"

"Basically, yes. My videos are what should count."

"But what if you've got it backwards?" He held her suspicious eyes. "Maybe you shouldn't worry so much about whether you and your videos are *seen* to be the same. Maybe you should be finding a way to make sure your videos *are* you."

"What exactly does that mean?"

"Tell me where you see your career going—TV? Feature films?"

She lowered her eyes to the fancy tray of hors d'oeuvres just set down by the waiter. As she meticulously picked out a small sculpture of vegetable and cheese, Fletcher thought he saw a brief, dark smile flit over her downturned face. He wondered if she intended to answer and if not, why not?

"I'm just living project to project. I know you'll find that very hard to believe since you probably had some very solid, long-range goals for Mercy from the beginning."

"My goal was always to keep her alive and sane while she built her career. Does that count?"

She resisted the chance to be flippant. "It does," she replied quietly. "Okay, I'll try to give you a straight answer. I've seen a lot of people catapulted into early success on the basis of…oh, beauty, connections, pure, idiotic luck. When it's not some quality within themselves that gets them there, and the craze that lifted them up *drops* them, they've got nothing to break their fall. So I don't allow myself to look ahead too much. I'm concentrating on *this* moment, *this* video. I'm building experience and, I hope, a professional reputation. Whether I ever get to do a *Gone With the Wind* or a *Star Wars* is irrelevant. I'll always be able to do *something*. Now," she said, drawing a breath and smiling to break the mood of gravity. "Why did you ask?"

"I guess it comes down to the question of whether you're satisfied by doing these documentaries. Are you?"

"Yes..." Her voice rose in a query, and her lashes flickered uncertainly. "I know they're not glamorous, but..."

"That's not it. Documentaries are the proper pursuit of a documentary maker. I just don't see you that way." Now *there* was a provocative comment; Fletcher shuddered to think he had just made it. If only she wouldn't overreact.

For a moment she seemed not to react at all. Then she sighed. "I know, you see me as a pressure cooker with the vent closed down, don't you?"

He laughed from relief and from the image itself. "If only because I know how it feels to be one. I was a very *restless* lawyer, remember. I'm just lucky I found something else to do...before I went boom!"

She raised her glass. "To not going boom!"

They drank this absurd, spontaneous toast in an agreeable mood that surrounded Fletcher like a band of light. This wasn't Carla's put-on stoicism; this was the genuine human being who lived deep inside, almost as deep, perhaps, as the wild, emotional creature he had stirred before. "So," he observed in what he hoped was a winning manner. "We *can* talk to each other after all."

"We must be learning the knack," she agreed, smiling a little self-consciously.

"Shall we see if we can dance?"

This time she blushed and his heart took an alarming lurch against his ribs. "All right."

She rose and let him take her hand, as shy as a girl on her first date—she couldn't bluff that away—her fingers were little blocks of ice while her palm burned. He had begun to feel a bit off-balance himself. When they reached the dance floor he faced her with the sincere intention of holding her at a decorous distance. Something else happened. His hand did not end up on cool, rustling fabric, it touched warm, silken skin—the dress had no back. He thought he felt her shiver when he touched her, but he couldn't be sure—his own reaction hit him too hard.

They danced for a few steps, or rather Fletcher felt he drifted on numbed legs, all sensation concentrated in the few square inches where they touched. A question from some long forgotten biology class popped into his mind—what part of the human body has the highest concentration of nerve endings? The hand, the fingertips.

He felt her float closer, pulled by arms under no conscious guidance of his own. It was like watching a Ouija board spell out some mysterious message: one's own hands pushed, but they knew not what they did. She came to rest against his chest, her head tucked under his chin, her cheek lightly pressed to his lapel. She exhaled so deeply, he realized she had been holding her breath.

This was senseless, even stupid. They had no basis for this closeness and no easy excuse such as being drunk. But he had no intention of letting her go.

At some point, after two hypnotic dances or twenty, he felt her shift slightly. "There's someone at our table."

Unwillingly, he swung around so he could see. "It's Rhoades, fashionably late as always." But not late enough, his senses insisted rebelliously. He had wanted to dance on and on, to dance off with her into the night and then...And then?

He disengaged himself from Carla, trying not to notice the flush that had spread over her porcelain neck and shoulders, and steadily headed them back to the table. Maybe Rhoades and his lady friend had come as saviors. Fletcher had never done anything unintentional in his life—until this troublesome and troubling girl appeared to throw him out of kilter, and he had been on the verge of letting the evening find its own course.

Rhoades, a rat-faced, jumpy man with fevered eyes, had on his arm the latest in a line of shapely, well-dressed, aspiring females. What they were aspiring to could be debated, but they all seemed to be named Heather or Jennifer or Julie. This one was Trudy. The only thing about her that caused Fletcher to take notice was the way Carla seemed to grow brittle when introduced. He had no time to puzzle over it.

"So this is the little filmmaker!" Rhoades effused, hanging on to Carla's hand.

Fletcher ground his teeth at the hand-holding and the greeting. He shot the record executive a look sharp enough to kill.

Rhoades caught it. "Don't worry, sweetie, Fletcher warned me that we were not to talk shop tonight, so I'll obey. This evening is purely for fun. And I can see it has great possibilities." He cast an unmistakable leer on Carla, who sat through it rigidly, looking like someone ready to dive overboard. "Ouch!" Rhoades bellowed. Startled, he looked accusingly at the perfectly bland Trudy. "Hey, you kicked me! Wow! I thought women's lib had taken care of that possessive stuff. Is yours giving you any trouble, Fletch?"

Carla's heartbeat tripped. "No, why?"

"You just look so familiar, and you're *doing* a film, right? Bobbie said something like that in the car coming up here."

"Yes, well, it's my own film—a video documentary. I don't work for anyone," she replied, trying to throw Trudy's not-too-keen mental powers off the track.

"But, I mean like, you never worked on a big film? I mean, I've been in a lot of productions—just little parts, but I've been told I'm good—and anyway, there always seem to be kids hanging out to learn the business—you know, as assistant to the director or something. I thought maybe I had seen you like that."

"No," Carla answered. "Whatever I know I learned at film school and on my own."

"Oh. Well..." Trudy passed from disappointment to her usual tame effervescence. "So you really are doing a film for Fletcher? I mean, you're not just dating him or something?"

At last Carla was able to laugh in true amusement. "No, I'm not dating him."

Trudy smiled brilliantly and threw Carla a look of affectionate relief. "Then you don't mind my saying he's the most gorgeous hunk of blond man I've ever laid my eyes on?"

"No, I don't mind. Don't worry, he's not *my* hunk of blond man and I have no designs on him." This was a good shift; perhaps Trudy would spend the rest of the evening fantasizing about Fletcher rather than wondering where she had seen Carla before. Or it *would* have been a good shift, if it had not bothered Carla almost as much.

They eventually had to return to the table—Carla felt Fletcher's acute gaze upon her across the entire room. When he rose to push in her chair for her, he stared at her so intensely that the back of her neck burned. She tried to make up for her previous antisocialness, knowing she was trying too hard. Her laughter was a little too bright, her talk a little too shallowly witty. Fletcher spent a lot of time frowning into his anisette.

Finally Rhoades made the only welcome statement of the evening, ''Well, kids, sorry to cut this short, but Trudy and I have to make an appearance at this boring little fete for one of our stockholders—a birthday or some other ghastly occasion. I wouldn't go, but I promised Trudy a look at that mausoleum of a house he's got out in the Hamptons.''

Trudy giggled and pressed his arm coyly. Whatever her speculative interest in Fletcher, she was obviously determined not to jeopardize Rhoades. Carla chastised herself, maybe she really cared for the awful little man....

Shortly thereafter she stood on the sidewalk with Fletcher watching the taillights of Rhoades's violet Mercedes veer around a corner. The breeze had grown cool enough that she had an excuse to pull her wrap tightly around her. Now what? she wondered.

Fletcher leaned against the restaurant's exterior brass railing, his golden hair glowing in the streetlight like some treasure in a showcase. He looked as if he might be formulating a dangerous question, so she forestalled him with one of her own. ''What was the point of this evening?''

''Somehow I'm getting used to your asking me that.''

''You keep setting up these incomprehensible situations to put me through. I never know why I'm in them.''

''Well, this one is really no mystery. Rhoades is a wheeler-dealer, his whole business consists of checking people out, making connections, seeing and being seen. You've just been added to his stock of potential talent.''

''Ugh. I don't like it.''

He smiled ironically and replied, ''It's the same thing I do, Carla. A lot of it is the same.''

"But," she countered anxiously, "you do it differently...or better...or something. There *is* a difference."

"Thank you for saying that."

She shivered. "No flattery intended, just the cool observations of a journalist—whether or not I'm a good one."

He smiled and looked off down the street. The breeze ruffled his angel-silk hair with a gentleness Carla could feel in her own fingertips. When he again looked back he *did* ask the dangerous question. "Forget Rhoades. Where are *we*? And don't ask me what I mean—you *know* what I mean."

Her gaze dropped away from his face and found a distraction in her own glittering shoes. "Where *can* we be?" She felt her words and her muscles stiffen protectively, grow cold. She couldn't help it, any more than she could help melting in his arms. "You put me in a tough situation, Fletcher. I'm still working for you, still relying on your goodwill in order to get my video done."

"You can't imagine that I'd expect..." He made a rough, inarticulate noise and struggled with a bitter smile. "Well, I guess that *is* the way the business works, isn't it? Pressure and favors, cashing in every advantage, bargaining with every attribute you've got. I'm sorry..."

The regret in his voice moved her uncontrollably. "I didn't mean to sound so harsh."

He waved her away. "No, you were just putting into words the rules I already live by. How can I blame you for that? I seem to remember harping on them over and over. It's ironic, actually."

He remained quiet for a few moments, his bemused gaze turned inward. Carla could think of nothing to say. She had a fervent desire to wrench him out of his glum mood, but didn't know how.

Before she had thought of anything, he pulled himself off the railing and gazed at her somberly. "You're right, we're exactly where we were. But you *have* my goodwill. Please know that. You don't need to do anything to get it.... Listen, can you get a cab for yourself?''

"Of course, but..."

"Then I'll be off. Good night, Carla." Without touching her or explaining himself, he turned and walked slowly out of sight down the half-lit street.

Chapter Seven

The heavy overcast sky suited Carla's mood the next morning when she launched herself out onto the street. The heat was oppressive and the clouds seemed to glower at her reproachfully. She hadn't slept well, sticking to the sheets no matter how she adjusted the air conditioning and seeing clearly in the forefront of her mind Fletcher's hurt posture last night.

In the gray light of day her guilt did not abate. She had treated him shabbily. If she had honestly meant to live by the cold words she had pronounced in front of him, she should not have danced with him in such a blissful trance. She would have guarded herself better from the very beginning. Was he so unreasonable to think their relationship might go beyond the professional? Not judging by her behavior, not unless he had ESP.

Yet he had yielded so generously, reproaching her with nary a word. He had agreed that her fears were natural; he hadn't tried to sway her with protestations that he was different somehow—trustworthy. Rather he had *proved* himself trustworthy by letting hers be the final word.

All of which made Carla severely reexamine what she had said and what she had meant. From the very first she hadn't known how to judge him; she had observed his behavior, listened to Dietra's babble and immediately called up a whole net of assumptions to catch him in. But he wasn't arrogant or insensitive at all. The extent of her misjudgment appalled her. She wanted to make it up to him—not for sake of their professional relationship, but for sake of his own good, gentle person.

Even the air in the Fifty-seventh Street building felt sticky. The sight of passing office workers in their suits or their dresses and nylon stockings made Carla grateful for her own loose blouse and shorts. Only Annette looked cool, one of her indispensable talents.

"Morning, Carla!" she called. "Is it raining out there yet?"

"No such luck, and I feel like a wad of old scrub rags."

"Yuck."

"So what's on the agenda today?" Carla asked in a falsely blithe tone. "I forgot to get instructions from Fletcher."

"Well, nothing, unless you want to follow Mercy and me to a MAY fundraising luncheon—have you a yen for shrimp aspic and cold chicken salad?"

"I'll pass. Isn't Fletcher going?"

"No, he's taking the late shift, doing a talk show on the opening of a shelter for runaways in Lower Manhattan. But until he has to leave he's lazing around in indolent luxury, enjoying his last bit of peace before we move to the new offices upstairs. Which reminds me—I have to see if the movers really *are* coming tomorrow or if they're going to cancel out again. Anyway, he *does* stop moving once in a while, you see.''

"I'll believe it when I see it.''

A new voice drawled from the interior of Fletcher's office. "I hear voices. I hope I'm not missing anything.'' Mercy undulated out of the doorway, stunning in a flower-skirted silk dress, her hair swirled into a French twist. She would have looked cool and chic, but at sight of Carla her expression grew hot and bothered. Her hello was barely civil. She deliberately plopped herself in a waiting-room chair and began flipping through a magazine, pointedly ignoring Carla.

Carla reminded herself not to be annoyed. "Since I've got no schedule I guess I'll just go then,'' she said to Annette. "Plenty of work back at the studio.''

"Oh, hey, wait!'' Annette frowned in sudden inspiration. "You know, it's rare to catch Fletcher at home, but you really should see the place if you're doing a documentary on him. You could even discuss setting up a day to tape a few sequences there.''

"Oh, I couldn't possibly bother him at home. . . .''

A sullen alto agreed from behind her. "I should say not! The *idea*, Annette.''

Annette paid no attention. "He wouldn't mind. Look, here's the address.'' She scribbled on a piece of paper. "It's not far. . . .''

The waves of disapproval from Mercy met Carla's own intense misgivings and made her refuse to take the paper. "Annette, I couldn't just barge in on him.''

The woman sighed. "Well, I know one way to convince you—I'll call him.''

Before Carla could frame a protest, Annette had punched the number into her phone and settled down to wait for an answer. "Fletcher! Four rings to get to the phone, you really must have been dozing off...Sure, tell me about it...Yes, we're all ready here. Mercy looks glorious. But you left a loose end here, you know...My confidence in you has just shattered. You've left your poor, hyperactive filmmaker without a subject today....Yeah, she's right here steaming mad at being so neglected...."

This made Carla wince.

Oblivious, Annette went on, "Anyway, I told her she should come over and see you in that gorgeous place of yours—the potentate enjoying his ill-gotten gains, so to speak. You two could thrash out some plans to tape an interview there or something.... Of course, I'm really getting into it—I'm the film half of this company, remember? ...Okay, I'll tell her....Bye." She hung up with a satisfied expression on her face. "He'll be there until three or so and he'll tell the doorman to expect you."

Mercy made a disgusted sound. Carla took the address in resignation.

Fletcher's building proved to be one of the grand old monsters along Central Park West in the Seventies, not far, in fact, from Chevrons. It had clearly been constructed during an age when architects had the freedom to build castles. Soot-darkened gray stone rose from the flagged sidewalk in glowering walls and brave, watchful turrets. Above them the main tower of the building rose in steps, each terrace fuzzy with the trees of rooftop gardens. Even that failed to weaken the overall aura of mystery and somber magic. It didn't seem to fit the bright, efficient Fletcher Arendt who wrote music contracts and calmed the storms of temperamental artists.

Yet it *did* suit him somehow. It suited the passion that lay concealed beneath his tailored surface, as currents were concealed beneath the shining face of the sea. This did nothing for Carla's self-possession; she felt as if she were entering a precinct where her old, familiar rules no longer applied. That, too, suited Fletcher.

"Ah, yes, Ms. Copeland!" the doorman exclaimed jovially. "Go on up, darlin'. He said to send you right through. Take the last elevator there past the fountain—he's all the way up at the top."

His warm welcome made Carla just a bit less conscious of her grubby, sweat-blotched clothing. The clean, fresh space of the foyer made her feel cooler. She walked delightedly through creamy marble halls with symmetrically grouped furniture upholstered in cool blues and grays and surrounded by potted trees.

Past the modest but bright little fountain, Carla found a brass-banded elevator, stepped in and pressed the penthouse button. The door opened moments later on an entirely different decor than that of the grand lobby. She saw before her a small landing with a hand-woven rya rug across the softly polished oak floor and an unvarnished pine table set with small cacti in pots. She recognized Fletcher's spare, sun-drenched taste and thought how cheerful and warm this would look in the dead of winter.

The foyer proved to be private; only one door led off from it and this stood open. She walked to the doorway, peered in and called "Fletcher?" There was no answer. Bolder, she stepped inside and examined the room. It was huge, as big as her whole studio. She hadn't seen such wide, open spaces since she last visited her parents' house. The pale oak floor continued throughout, as did the sand-colored rugs. Large skylights sifted the soft glow of sunlight onto a couple of groupings of furniture—one a simple reading area with comfortable-looking chairs and standing lamps, the other a cluster of Moroccan-cotton couches set around a low table made from the cross section of an enormous tree. On the walls hung subtly colored Navajo rugs and very large, muted paintings by a Hopi artist whose work she knew. Cacti in rough clay pots provided the rest of the decoration. The room was sparse, but balanced and inviting. She came in farther, still looking for Fletcher.

The group of couches faced a wide stretch of sliding glass doors out onto one of the terraces she had noted from below, and there she finally located Fletcher. He lay stretched out on a wooden chaise, eyes closed, his golden skin exposed to the cloud-covered sun except for that covered by a pair of extremely faded denim cutoffs. Carla selfishly used the opportunity to run her eyes over his sleek, radiant body. People joined health spas in the usually vain hope of acquiring such bodies. Fletcher apparently came by his the same way he came by his business talent—naturally. Jealously, she thought of her hours of sweaty workouts designed to make up for her own pocket-size build.

She rapped on the door pane—no response. Then she realized that he was wearing little headphones and probably couldn't hear her. The thick heat of the outside world rolled in when she slid open the doors. She picked up a wooden chip that had strayed from one of the tree planters and fired it at Fletcher, hitting him squarely on his broad chest. He languidly removed the phones from his ears and replied without opening his eyes, "Hello, Carla." At least he was smiling.

"Many people would think you're nuts for lying out here when there's no sun."

"Ah, but those would be the people who had forgotten science class in elementary school, where they learned that ultraviolet rays come through the clouds."

Carla was one of those people, so she sidled onto another subject. "So you think that's a good enough reason to be lazing around having fun while Annette is out there slaving?''

"I protest!" he said, finally opening his slanted eyes. "Come here and listen to this, *then* tell me if I'm having fun."

The friendliness of his manner gave her hope that he might not think her an impossibly hardhearted cynic. She happily walked out and sat on the side of the chaise by his long legs. She endured the headphones only a minute before she returned them with a grimace. "What *is* that? It sounds like a fork caught in a garbage disposal."

"It's an audition tape sent by a band called the Men in the Moon. Here's their letter."

Carla read a note scrawled in disjointed handwriting. "Mr. Arendt, We decided, after you signed Billy P., that you just might have an ear for really potent rock 'n' roll. I mean, he's still a little fluffy, but what a step up from the Riley pigeon. If you really want to make sociological, musicological and cosmological history, we are your band—The Men."

Carla exclaimed, "They must be kidding!"

"And I've got thirty-five more tapes to wade through back at the office."

"Why do you bother? I take it these are unsolicited tapes."

"Unsolicited and unbelievable. But how would you feel if you sent me a tape that represented your total artistic accomplishment—and you included return postage—and it went directly into my trash can?"

She cleared her throat, "Uh, actually..."

Fletcher frowned, "Now that videotape of my office door doesn't count—unless you claim it represents your total artistic accomplishments."

"Not exactly."

"Well, then. I listen to them, but I then feel perfectly free to send out cordial form letters telling them that their music is obviously sincere, but I am totally booked up."

"Have you ever found anybody good this way?"

"Once. She just opened a musical off-Broadway, as a matter of fact. So one out of twenty thousand..."

"And you'll take the odds."

"Sure, you never give up trying, hoping. Though it's a bit like beating your head against a wall."

"I distinctly remember hearing you say you weren't a masochist."

"No, I'm not! I'm an *optimist*. I *hope* there's a difference."

The first splat of rain landed on Carla's head. She looked up at the leaden sky and said, "Well, finally! Now maybe it'll cool off." Then she scrambled for the shelter of the living room, Fletcher an agile split second behind her. Even as they slid the door shut, the rain changed from droplets to sheets. The terrace swam with water.

"Oh, your tape player!" Carla remembered in horror. But of course Fletcher had managed to scoop it up and bring it with him. Quite in contrast to Annette's accusation, he *never* left loose ends. Considering this, why *had* he arranged to be lying around sunbathing when he knew she was going to show up? Awareness of his closeness at that moment overwhelmed her. His amber skin seemed to have absorbed whatever sun had gotten through the clouds and then brought it with him into the apartment. Heat and a tantalizing scent filtered from him, a healthy, outdoorsy musk that, since she moved to the city eight years earlier, Carla had quite forgotten existed.

She skittered clear of his presence, daunted by her own raw nerves. She had come over specifically to be pleasant to him and make up for the previous night, but now she wondered how she had planned to keep within the bounds of such a bland intention. "You have a gorgeous place, Fletcher," she chattered inanely. "Have you lived in the southwest?"

"Yes, that's where I'm from—New Mexico." At her surprised expression, he cocked a mocking eyebrow. "Why? Did you think I was some sewer rat from the Bronx perhaps?"

"No, I...uh...well, actually that would explain you better. Somehow I don't think of New Mexico as the best school for street smarts like you've got."

"I suppose I've just always had a sneaky turn of mind. We're not all country half-wits roaming around the desert with our mouths hanging open, you know. The desert's a dangerous place if you don't know what you're doing. Sometimes even if you do."

She gestured at the trappings of the room. "But you must think it's beautiful. You brought it with you to live in. Or do you just have a cactus fetish?"

"Ah, there's a theme for your documentary—Fletcher Arendt's search for the sweet flesh beneath the thorns."

"I do see the similarity between cacti and some of the people you work with."

"I thought you would."

"Mercy jumps immediately to mind."

Fletcher nodded. "She's one of them."

"Something's been bothering me, Fletcher...I know you wanted me to teach her a little bit about the video business, but I'm not making any headway."

He sighed in resignation. "I'm not surprised. It was kind of a vain hope. She's very headstrong, unlike us reasonable folk."

"As long as you know I *have* tried to be conscientious."

"Conscientious Carla." He smiled. "That's why I hired you. I'm going to rustle up some grub, as they say around the camp fires of my native land...."

"Don't exaggerate. I'll bet you're from Santa Fe or some other *city* in New Mexico, right?"

"Gallup, but don't evade the issue. Speaking of Mercy, as we were, she just gave me a cookbook—how to prepare haute cuisine with low intelligence, or something like that. I'm up to page one-fifty—peanut butter-and-jelly sandwiches. How hungry are you?"

"I think it's a question of how *brave*."

"Well!" He dusted his hands theatrically and treated her to a manic grin. "We've already established that you're *brave*. Follow me."

He led her into a kitchen of oak and rough, Spanish clay tiles. It was cozy rather than small and lacked only a little breakfast table by the low-silled window. She wondered fleetingly where Fletcher coaxed himself awake in the morning—here at the counter or in the living room? Did he snuggle back into bed with a cup of coffee or was he one of those revolting beings who woke fully the minute they opened their eyes? She groaned. Then, at Fletcher's concern, she continued melodramatically. "Food! I'm famished!"

The peanut butter and jelly turned out to be almond butter and honey and the bread was fresh whole wheat, not Fletcher's own work, he assured her. He cut up red peppers and rounded out the meal with cold milk and grapes.

"I must admit," Carla reflected, holding her stuffed belly. "This is the closest I've come to real nutrition since I left home. I mean, I always try to eat good food, but I never quite manage *meals*. I guess it's not having a kitchen..."

Fletcher closed the door on the dishwasher and no trace remained that the kitchen had been used. He was so efficient, what a great wife he would make....

"Where do you live?" he demanded.

"I live in my studio," she replied, enjoying his look of disbelief. "Don't tell anyone though—it's only zoned commercial and my landlord would get in big trouble. Plus I'd have to move."

"I have a vivid picture of you stretched out with your head on a camera."

"It was like that at the beginning. I had a real apartment in Brooklyn—three bedrooms and two roommates, but I was hardly ever there. I'd work till three in the morning and then there was really no sense in calling the car service. Eventually I hauled in a couple of foam mattresses and finally I gave up on the apartment altogether. So all this," she indicated the entirety of his apartment, "is unbelievable domestic luxury to me."

"What if someday you want to entertain business associates or something? Or is that too frivolous for a serious filmmaker?"

"And I came over here to be *nice* to you!"

His eyes widened. "Oh, did you? I thought you were checking out another set for your video."

Carla sat there feeling the heat rise in her face. "I'm damned whatever I say, aren't I?"

"I don't know—say something."

She had started it now. He sat solidly before her, clearly unwilling to be lured on to another subject. Carla stared at the smooth oak counter to avoid his expectant eyes. "Well...it occurred to me after last night that I might seem a bit...callous. I know I go on and on about professionalism and all, but I hoped you might forgive that and..."

"See beneath the thorns?" he suggested gently. His smile warmed her, chased away some of the skittish feeling she had at exposing any of herself to a man who could get through her defenses so easily.

"That's my specialty, remember?" he continued, taking a half step back from their touchy intimacy, still as warm but less dangerous. "Brrr...I think all this air conditioning and cold food is getting to me. I'm going to put on a shirt."

He had pulled away from her on his own; she didn't know whether she should be relieved or hurt. She checked herself—she had come over to make up for *her* behavior, not to find more excuses to misjudge him. If he wanted to keep a little distance between them after the huge chasm she had dug last night, it was his right. She sternly arranged her feelings so they wouldn't affect her next words. "You do very well with Mercy. I've seen that. She has a temper that could kill."

"She does, indeed." He chuckled, disappearing through the kitchen door. To hear the rest of his remark, Carla scurried after him. "But to be fair, you're seeing her at a particularly trying time—she's got to go on the road and face big audiences with a lot of untried material. She's terrific in front of an audience and she thrives on it, but she's got horrid stage fright."

"I can believe all that, but somehow I can't imagine that she's ever truly placid and easygoing." She followed him down a shadowy hall.

"Oh, no!" Fletcher agreed. "And I wouldn't *want* her to be, even if it would make life easier. She's one of those artists who needs to be all nerves half the time—you've heard her sing; you know what kind of passion she's got."

As much as it irked Carla to see Mercy in such a favorable light, she knew Fletcher spoke the strict truth. A calm Mercy would be a dull Mercy.

Fletcher turned from the hallway into a large room, its stillness broken by the patter of rain on the window glass—his bedroom. Carla had not allowed herself to think about where they might be headed, but where else would Fletcher get a shirt? She skidded to a halt at the doorstop and listened while he finished his remark from inside a walk-in closet. "I've never seen it as my job to keep her calm, as I've said before, just alive." He returned, slipping a pale yellow shirt over his bronzed arms. He saw her hanging back at the doorway and chidingly, astutely, said, "Chicken."

She promptly lifted her chin and walked firmly to the center of the room. "Why, Fletcher, what courage could I possibly need? I have perfect trust in you."

"That's a mistake," he remarked, buttoning the cuffs and stepping closer.

She knew he did it to taunt her and so refused to flinch. "We've already settled this anyway. We agreed that there are too many complications standing in the way of..." She stopped short.

"Of?"

"Of anything. Anyway, we went through this already." She mumbled this last looking down, still not willing to meet his eyes.

"Remember, I claim to be an optimist."

"You wouldn't go back on our understanding, would you?"

"Not by myself," he murmured, closing the last bit of distance between them. "If you're still here in ten seconds, though, I'm going to kiss you."

"I think we've established a nice working relationship...."

"Five seconds."

"...And it would really be contrary to the spirit of it..."

And so he kissed her, as he had said, as she had known he would. He cupped her face in his big, gentle hands and stopped her words with his silent lips. She had feared both extremes of her reaction to him. Coldness felt so cruel and so wrong; this ready heat felt terrifyingly inevitable. He had given her an adequate—no, quite generous—opportunity to leave and she had purposely frittered it away. Now she was caught, fluttering half off balance, feeling his fingers sliding down her throat and playing with the rim of her collar. Entranced, she waited for him to pull her into the golden circle of his arms and to open her mouth with his kiss.

Instead he dragged himself away and looked at her through hypnotic eyes. "I wasn't entirely honest with you, Carla—I only said I'd *kiss* you. But you know what I want—I want to make love with you."

She had banished thought, afraid of what her mind would tell her. But Fletcher pulled her out of that dreamlike suspension with his next words. "It's up to you. Yes?"

Fear answered for her. "No."

The second after she said it she felt herself dragged by the hand out of the bedroom. It seemed Fletcher could not leave those surroundings quickly enough. He pulled her determinedly through the hall and released her once they reached the neutrality of the living room. He paced frenetically for a moment, then yanked open the sliding glass doors and threw himself out into the pelting rain.

Carla's breathing had barely steadied. Her cry of "Fletcher!" was less than a gasp; he couldn't have heard it and wouldn't have responded if he had. Suddenly her mind cleared. All the nonsense tangling her in nets of confusion and indecision melted away like spiderwebs in the rain. She hadn't meant a sound of that spontaneous "no." She had meant "yes" with all her heart. There *was* no safe way for her and Fletcher, and she no longer had the will to protect herself from the danger.

Yet she had ruined it. For once in her life she wished she had not been allowed to make her own choice. It was a miserable thing to realize; it contradicted every requirement she had ever made of life—for independence and strength and control. But she wished with every drop of her being that Fletcher had taken the decision away and carried her those few steps to his bed.

Instead there he sat on the chaise, arms wrapped tightly around his knees, eyes staring intently at nothing, rain fusing the yellow shirt to his skin.

Carla shivered with the turbulence of emotions too long pent up. This time she would have no chance to sit with remorse and walk blithely back into his life ready to absorb his forgiveness, his sunny friendship. If she wanted to save any good from the shambles she had made, her only chance was now.

"Fletcher," she said surely, loudly enough to be heard over the thunder of rain. He refused to look up; she thought she saw the small muscles in his jaw tighten. She stepped out into the downpour and walked quietly across the flooding terrace. When she had come within arm's length of him, he growled a warning, still not looking at her, "Don't do this to me again, Carla."

Guilt stabbed her. She had pulled away from him so many times, yet now, when he could have been reproachful or cruel, he held himself down to this one measured entreaty.

Surer than ever of the feeling that moved her, she sat on the edge of the chaise beside him, felt a little spark of amusement at how he struggled to keep his eyes directed straight ahead. Then, echoing his own touch long minutes ago, she took his face in her hands and kissed him softly on the mouth.

His eyes were full of thunderclouds, just like the sulky sky; his voice was raw with emotion. "There's no point in this, Carla."

She kept her face close to his, marveling at the heat that rose from him in the chill air. Raindrops jeweled his lashes and sparkled on his hot gold skin—she wondered why they didn't steam. Against his cheek she murmured, "I thought you wanted to make love with me."

His eyes focused on her now, cross and suspicious. "And I thought you said no."

"I never told you," she explained, burying her fingers in the darkening strands of his wet hair. "I have a history of insanity."

He blinked momentarily, then a clear light broke through the storm in his eyes. His arms went around her back, inflexible as steel straps. Dragging her across his lap, he murmured, "I always suspected as much."

Those were the last words either of them spoke for the next several moments. Carla lost herself in the delicious strength of Fletcher's embrace. She let him lower her back to the cushions, concerned only that she didn't lose the sweet contact with his mouth. He wrapped his leg behind her knees and locked her thighs to his. The arm that rested beneath her shoulders dropped her head back and exposed her neck to his exploring lips. While his teeth nipped down the line of her jaw, she felt his free hand whisper over the wet fabric plastered to her waist. His fingers traced her lower ribs to the untucked hem of her blouse and she flushed, anticipating the feel of his fingers on her skin. He stroked her waist softly, lingeringly, until she longed for him to be bolder. Her body cried out for rapture and passion. In desperation she found his mouth again and bit him.

After the surprise cleared his eyes narrowed in comprehension. In one fluid move he shifted until he lay directly over her, legs interwoven with her legs, hips seductively heavy on hers. His caressing hand, no longer shy, skimmed under the wet blouse and lit a trail of fire through her nerves. He plucked up the soft edge of her lacy bra and his light fingers swept tormentingly over her nipple, raising from her a breathless groan. His open palm cupped her breast, fitting it as perfectly as her mouth fit his. How could she have waited so long for this? Why hadn't she known that first blazing moment when she saw him at the head of the stairs at Weeds that she was meant to live in his arms, drunk on his spirit, destroyed and reformed in the furnace of his passion? She had kept so much from him—her love and her truth. All those loathsome evasions boiled up from her memory like an ugly sludge.

When he broke off his kiss for breath she whispered, "Fletcher?"

He answered with a soft, wordless sound and nibbled her lower lip.

She forced herself to remember that she wanted to speak. "There are so many things I've never told you..."

"I'm finding out what I need to know."

She struggled on. "But all this time you must have thought I was a raving lunatic."

"Maybe a little," he agreed, dusting kisses on her cheeks and eyelids. "But I'm very attracted to raving lunatics."

"Can we be serious for just a minute?"

"My love, we are well on our way to being *very* serious."

She sighed in acquiescence and let his tongue sweep the words from her mouth. But the thought pricked her insistently. "Fletcher?"

Finally he rose up on his elbows, still close enough that her every breath swelled against his chest. He managed a look of indulgent resignation. "I'm attracted to *stubborn* raving lunatics. Okay, go ahead—you're wanted for murder, right?''

"Well, it's not quite so bad, but...I'm not exactly...my background is a little problematic. I was afraid if I told you who I was you wouldn't treat me like a normal person.''

"You're *not* a normal person.''

"Listen! I don't mean just you in particular—*everybody*. I've always wanted to be taken on my own merits and you know how glamour-struck people are in music and in film.... And when I learned that Mercy had movie ambitions I was extra nervous....''

"You must be extranervous *now;* you're babbling.''

She was, indeed, she realized and struggled to collect her thoughts into one sentence. "My mother is Amelia Abbott-Copeland, the movie producer.''

The silence terrified her. His expression did not change, until he finally frowned in exasperation. "*That's* what you had to tell me? *That's* what bothered you so much you couldn't concentrate? I must be totally losing my touch.''

Amazed, she felt him bend down to her again and drown her in a kiss that obliterated every other concern. He pulled her more urgently against him and crushed out all possibility of speech. The rain vanished from her consciousness and all the world was his honey breath, his taste and his imperative body.

Until a sharp beep sounded in her ear—his wristwatch alarm. "Damn!'' he swore explosively. To her dismay he wrenched himself upright, leaving her cold and sodden on the chaise.

"What's that for?''

"It's to remind me that I'm still somehow connected to the rest of the world, however easy it is to forget that in your presence. I have to get showered and dressed for an idiotic talk show.''

"Oh, yeah..." She dragged herself up, suddenly aware of how wet she was and how incomplete she felt separated from him. But she wouldn't burden him with her misery—he would remember in a moment, as she had, that this talk show was in support of his much-loved project, MAY.

Recovering his spirits somewhat, he leaned down and kissed her on the forehead. "Come inside and I'll wrap you up in a big warm robe so you don't shiver yourself to splinters."

She obeyed gladly, holding his hand. His bedroom held no fears for her now, just wistful regrets. As he promised, he bundled her in his own fluffy terry-cloth robe and set to work toweling her hair. She pushed him away teasingly. "I'll be all right. Go get ready. I don't want anyone to accuse me of interfering with your work."

He rolled his eyes. "As if you can help it!" Then he disappeared into the bathroom and shortly she heard the running shower. Her wet clothes stuck to her unpleasantly; she wanted to take them off and snuggle beneath the soft quilts of his bed, but reflected that this might not encourage him to get ready in time. He popped out of the bathroom again as if he had heard her thoughts. "It's going to be very hard to keep my mind on teenage runaways, thinking how I let *you* escape."

She wrinkled her nose at him, hoping this wasn't too provocative. He continued in a suggestive tone, "Of course, you *could* be here when I get home...."

"And what time will that be?"

A disgusted look transformed his face. "About midnight...there's a reception after the taping of the show. I never noticed before, but this PR stuff is just *endless*...I guess you'd better go home and wait...grrr..."

"I'll see you tomorrow—what do you have planned?"

"Nothing I can't put off for as long as necessary," he promised.

"Well," she said, jumping up and handing him his damp robe. "You're getting very unprofessional, Fletcher Arendt. I'd better go home before you decide you can put off this talk show. Go on now—you're going to run out of hot water."

He groaned again. "I didn't turn on the *hot* water."

She giggled, kissed his nose and left him to his work.

Chapter Eight

The previous day's thunderstorm had cooled and cleaned the city streets. Carla felt her emotions as fresh and glittering as the weather, and she bounded to Fifty-seventh Street with a light heart. No camera today—she suspected that if Fletcher had time for her as a camera crew that day he'd have time for her as a woman. For the first time in her life that was more important.

She had picked up Adrian's gold dress from the dry cleaners and returned it to the designer, trying to keep some of the giddiness out of her voice as she expressed her thanks.

"Hmmm," Adrian had remarked slyly. "Looks like the great Fletcher Arendt is not impervious to my sartorial talents."

"Perhaps not entirely," Carla had admitted.

"Uh-uh! Well, you have no idea what you've done for my self-confidence, my dear."

"Oh, I have an idea." But Carla would not discuss it further, despite Adrian's curiosity, and had to be quite firm with the woman in order to be allowed to leave.

The storm outside seemed to have been echoed by one inside Arendt Management. The doors had been thrown open and all through the reception area were piled large cardboard cartons that trailed lamp cords and dirt from the cacti. Annette sat on the floor, holding the one telephone still plugged in, and directed movers while she scribbled notes on her phone pad.

"Remember, the *black* file cabinets go in Mr. Arendt's office, the *gray* ones in *mine*.... Now what was that, Andy? The promoter says he's *not* going to supply vegetarian food for the band?"

Oh, yes, Carla remembered, moving day. Other concerns had driven it out of her head—and Fletcher's.

Annette waved her in. "No, tell him tuna salad is *not* acceptable, I want *tofu*...Hi, Carla, Fletcher's upstairs on the thirtieth floor.... No, Andy, I did not sneeze. It's a kind of food—T-O-F-U! Right, bean curd...Okay, let me know what the creep says. Bye." She massaged her temples with a weary hand.

Mercy's languid voice floated in from the room that had held the large pile of cartons ever since Carla had first walked into Arendt Management. "Of course he has to move in the middle of my tour preparations! I don't know *where* he gets his ideas!" She flipped idly through a music magazine. Although she wore a simple plaid shirt and worn jeans, she looked as if lifting a box was the last thing she'd require of her long-nailed hands.

"Be fair, Mercy!" Annette pleaded. "The movers canceled out on us twice. Fletcher can do wonders, but even he is no match for union movers. What are you standing around for, Carla? You should be taping this...." A grimy young man stepped over Annette, the box in his arms barely clearing her head. " 'Chaos strikes Fletcher Arendt...' "

"Actually, if he's that busy, I probably shouldn't bother him at all." Her heart sank at the prospect.

Mercy drawled with venomous sarcasm. "He's always got time for *you*, sugar—for all the good it ever does anybody...."

Annette shushed her and the singer sourly retreated into the storeroom. "Never mind her, Carla. Fletcher's been distracted since yesterday and she thinks the world is ending."

So Fletcher had been distracted, had he? Carla couldn't keep a grin from her face. "Well, maybe I will go up, see the new place..."

"Yes, do! There's something on the door that *I'm* particulary proud of." Annette showed the first flush of emotion that Carla had ever observed in her.

"Well, it must be something if it's gotten a reaction out of you. I'm on my way."

As Carla followed the trail of dropped paper clips out the door, she heard Mercy emerge from the storeroom and comment in a whisper obviously meant to be overheard, "Stop shushing me, Annette! He's just wasting his time— she's never going to do us the good of a flea on a fur coat...."

This puzzled Carla for a moment, but she put it out of her mind. It was no secret that Mercy disliked her for taking up Fletcher's precious time. Well, she'd have to get used to it. Carla had the feeling she'd be taking up more and more of it.

She climbed the fire stairs in order to stay clear of the movers. On the thirtieth floor a line of dusty footprints and lost index cards led her to the new office. Carla stepped aside for a man carrying a tope chair and noticed the sign before her. So *that* was what Annette had meant! On huge, smooth doors of velvety white oak, burnished bronze letters spelled out "Arendt/Harrow Management Enterprises Ltd." Arendt/*Harrow*! He had made Annette his partner! Now at least her devotion would be officially recognized for the world; people could no longer think of her as Fletcher's underling. *He* never had, but Carla had seen the long-suffering Annette treated as a secretary too many times not to feel smug for her now.

The reception area was bigger than the old one, and instead of two doors opening off it, there were four reached from a short, wide hallway with a big, sunny window at the end. Arendt/Harrow must be doing well, Carla decided, if even their new hall had a window. Behind the first door she found a large room piled with crates of stereo and video equipment and soft squishy couches—a multimedia conference room. The next door closed on two storage rooms, then came Annette's spacious office—with gray *and* black file cabinets in it, Carla noted—and lastly, facing Annette's across the hall window, was Fletcher's suite.

Carla ducked two movers who emerged like rampaging bulls, and then peeked in. Fletcher, dressed in a sleeveless gray T-shirt that set afire the polished gold of his muscular arms, stood over the desk setting up his computer terminal. It was clear from the gloss on his skin that he had been doing heavier work as well. Every tiny, controlled ripple that moved beneath that perfect skin Carla felt as electricity through her own body. She paused in the doorway, enjoying the sight of him.

As if he felt the intensity of her gaze, he looked up. A sly smile lit his face. "I just figured out how to christen my new office," he remarked.

"How's that?"

"Come here and I'll show you."

She sauntered in slowly; it wouldn't do to inflate his ego *too* much by jumping into his arms. She deliberately stopped so that the desk separated them and then she casually leaned one hip against the edge. This neither fooled nor inconvenienced Fletcher—he simply swept her into his arms, pulled her clear across the desktop and kissed her thoroughly. "Ah, now the place feels like home."

At that moment a potbellied mover entered and dropped his end of a long couch. He eyed Fletcher and Carla coolly, muttered a gruff "Uh-huh" and stomped out.

Fletcher grinned apologetically at Carla. "Well, maybe not exactly like *home*...although I could lock the door...."

From the hallway, near the hidden end of the couch, came a laconic observation, "If we go into overtime today, you won't like the bill, Mr. Arendt."

Carla smothered her giggles in Fletcher's shoulder. He gave a disgruntled growl and helped her swing herself to her feet. "We're really going to have to work on our timing, Fletcher."

"*Our* timing is fine—it's the entire rest of the universe that's getting in the way." His cross expression amused her. She felt so happy to be with him in this new atmosphere of possibilities that the presence of a thousand interfering movers wouldn't have phased her.

"Well, the sooner we get your new office semiorganized, the sooner you'll be able to take a well-deserved rest, right?"

"Rest?" he pouted. "You must not think I'm very exciting."

She threw a roll of tape at him. "Don't get technical on me, Mr. Arendt. I was just about to offer my services as an office organizer, which is really above and beyond the call of duty for a poor measly filmmaker."

"I can hardly turn down unpaid help. It beats union overtime. And maybe we'll be able to sneak away from here before the rest of my work catches up with me."

"So, where do I start?"

"Find the box that says 'desk junk.'"

"Yes, sir," she saluted smartly.

They spent a companionable, if exhausting, morning second-guessing the movers and finding boxes that had strayed into unexplored reaches of the suite. Although most of the time they attended closely to business, Carla thoroughly enjoyed working with Fletcher. These hours duplicated the best of their times together, talking and exchanging views, and now there was the added spice of new romance. Fletcher found every possible chance to pass by and nibble on her neck or tickle her. She had to severely discipline herself to stick to her work.

Just before lunchtime Fletcher's newly installed phone rang. He scrambled through the unpacked confusion to find it and answered, "Ah, hello, Bob..."

Carla continued to arrange a file drawer, wondering if this was the offensive Bob Rhoades.

"Well, you found her, all right. Hang on." He punched the hold button and called Carla. "It's your favorite dinner companion, Bob Rhoades. He says he's been calling your studio all morning in an absolute *fever* to get hold of you."

She made a face. "I never gave him my number."

"*I* did. He's a potential employer for you, after all."

"Yuck. What's he want anyway?"

"Maybe he wants you to make a movie of his life."

"Send him that tape of your doorway."

"Come on, stubborn love of my life. He can't help it if he's only three-quarters human."

Reluctantly she took the phone. Fletcher snatched a kiss and then gave her a second to recover before he released the hold button.

"Mr. Rhoades? This is Carla Copeland."

"Honey, *Bob*, please! We survived an entire dinner together under the baleful glare of Kaiser Arendt!" His pushy enthusiasm caused her jaws to lock. "It's a bond for life, doll."

She made no reply.

Undaunted, he pressed on. "All this talk of food—listen, sweetie—why don't you let me buy you lunch? I've got a little business to rake over with you."

"About the video?"

"Video? Oh, you mean this thing for Fletch. Nah, that's small stuff compared to what I'm talking about. I'm just about to run out to the Fountainbleu—it's right around the corner from you on Sixth Avenue. Meet me there in, say, twenty minutes. Tell that Casanova Arendt that he's not invited. I want you all to myself."

"Actually, I've got other plans."

"If I know Fletcher's work habits, that means burritos out of a greasy paper bag. Come on, live a little! Twenty minutes, huh?" Without waiting for any more argument, he hung up.

Carla glared at the phone, exasperated. "That man has a colossal nerve! He assumes I'm ready to drop everything to run off and have lunch with him."

"Hmm..." Fletcher remarked darkly.

"He says he's got business to discuss. Do you suppose he does?"

Fletcher chuckled. "Actually, yes. He's been checking up on your progress all along, you know. Of course, I've praised you to the skies, liar that I am...ouch! Don't throw the office around, we just got it set up!"

"Be serious here! That obnoxious man can't possibly offer me anything I want to work on."

"The same thought crossed my mind when your friend Dietra turned up as the mover behind your documentary, you know. No personal offense to her..."

"I know she is a bit hard to take sometimes."

"So you see my point—Rhoades may *propose* a project, but you can bet he's got nothing to do with it on a workaday basis. You might get to work with good people. Perhaps none as fascinating as me but..."

"I'd *better* go, just to shut you up."

The Fountainbleu, in contrast to its grand name, turned out to be a snobby little hole in the wall guarded by a stiletto-mustached man with an exaggerated French accent and a supercilious manner. It pleased Carla greatly that even though she wore an old shirt and jeans with bleach marks, he didn't dare keep her out once she told him Rhoades expected her. She wondered, however, if he might not have had the last word by hiding her at a dark, semihidden table.

Ready for Rhoades to saunter in late, she ordered a bourbon. How impulsive she had become, falling in love with Fletcher, telling him her greatest secret, ordering liquor in the middle of the day. Perhaps it was time to let go of a few old inhibitions, the reserve that cemented her insides. When she had suffered through this pointless ordeal with Rhoades, she intended to drag Fletcher back to his apartment, unplug the phones and throw his wristwatch over the terrace wall.

Rhoades came by himself this time and he seemed even more inconsequential and irritating without a beautiful woman on his arm to distract one's attention. To her horror, he splattered a rapid kiss on her face as he scraped his chair around to crowd hers. "Doll, you came to your senses and showed up! Great! Will you look at this cruddy table they gave us? I'll have to have a talk with the bum that runs the place. I give this dump a lot of business. What's that—whiskey?'' He beckoned the waiter with a loud snap of his fingers. Carla cringed. ''Bring me a Beefeater's straight up, okay? Oh, my ulcers…''

Carla found her mind empty of even the dumbest social comments. Fortunately, the rat-faced record exec allowed no awkward silences to fall between them. ''Say, Carla honey, you've gotta have the chicken liver stuff. It's wildly overpriced, but it really is the best grub on the menu. Live a little, right? It's the company's money—Mercy Riley's money, you could say!'' He chortled. ''Speaking of the diva, how are you getting on with Fletcher?''

''Fine.'' Carla hoped that by keeping to monosyllables she might be able to avoid telling Rhoades what she thought of him.

''*Fine,* huh? Ha-ha! I'll have to tell him that—most ladies find they have a bit more to say about him than 'fine.' Ha-ha! He'll turn blue…or green or whatever color his royal blood is!''

She didn't even blink when he ordered for her. If he wanted to order the most expensive dish on the menu and then watch it lie cold on her plate he was welcome to do so.

He managed to spout enough useless conversation for the two of them until the soup came. Carla felt a bit warm from the bourbon and, with every passing moment, more impatient to get back to the more agreeable warmth of Fletcher's arms. Finally she felt she might have to take a hold of Rhoades's throat and wrench from him what this tedious lunch was all about. ''I know you're taking me out just to be nice.'' She writhed at saying this. ''But I remember your saying you had business to 'rake over' with me.''

"Ah, yeah, *business.* So I do. Hey, Fletch said you were a serious little thing—very dedicated. I like that. You've been in this business how long? I mean as a *filmmaker?*"

This phrasing sent prickles up Carla's spine for some reason, but otherwise it sounded like the standard opening of something like a job interview. "Four years," she answered. "Plus four years in film school."

"Well, then, with that and your background you probably have a good feel for how things work in the industry."

With that and her background? The prickles made her hair rise off the nape of her neck.

"I've got a little proposition for you, Carla. It'll do us both a lot of good. Sound has a big video budget—we do a lot of promo spots for our artists, and we can always use talent. I'm not talking about a staff position, I realize you like to work as an independent, but I know I can throw free-lance work your way at a pretty steady pace. Enough to keep you in hotdogs, that's for sure." He laughed. Carla waited grimly. It sounded as if the point of the whole monologue was only moments away.

Rhoades splashed through some soup, practically gargling his next words. "I've been reading in the trade papers that your mother's financing a new, big-budget flick. Now I know she's months away from the fun work, like choosing a composer for the soundtrack and the recording artists, the label, that whole bit, but I wanted to sneak in while the field was still open...."

Carla had gone rigid. He *knew.* That Trudy person must have scraped the old gum off her brain and remembered. *This* was why Carla had stuck to being Carla Copeland. At least it was the nastier part of the reason. It was all fine and noble to want to make it on her own merits, but if that wasn't enough, there were always favor-grabbers around, people who started to salivate at the prospect of getting an "in" with the mighty Amelia. Just as well she had told Fletcher herself, before it trickled back to him through this sponger.

"Now, I think we've been pretty good to you at Sound. Maybe you'll do us a little favor—drop a few words into Mom's ear so she thinks of us when the time comes. We've got a *dynamite* artist roster, all styles, all tastes."

Frigidly, Carla replied, "Mr. Rhoades, I assure you my mother's business is entirely separate from me. We are mother and daughter, not colleagues exchanging favors and expensive lunches."

Immediately the man's genial manner fell away, exposing the ruthless instincts that had shaped his ferrety face. "Come on, honey, be nice. It's not as if there weren't two million other camera jockeys out there who could do the work."

Carla was about to declare her utter indifference to any work he cared to offer her, but he rampaged on.

"I say we've been good to you—I'll make that a little more clear—we've bent over backward for you. It's damn lucky for you your pal Sharpe mentioned your mom's name to me. You think Fletcher Arendt *wanted* some fluffy-headed gal sticking a camera in his face while he was getting two big tours on the road? Fat chance. He would have dumped you and your camera in the back alley if I hadn't impressed upon him the fact that you had more to you than your artistic pretensions. He *can* be made to see reason, especially when it's to his own and his precious Mercy's advantage. So don't flatter yourself that he just likes your cute face. Neither Fletcher nor me is that simpleminded."

And she had thought Fletcher's reaction to her revelation remarkably calm! No wonder; it had been no news to him. She thought of all the times her temper had driven her to what must have seemed inexplicable behavior, or when it had exploded, making her nearly give away her secret. She thought of Fletcher's nearly unflappable patience. He had taken her abuse time after time and come back again, sweet-talking her with his looks, his words, his hands. So who had been the better actor?

Without realizing it, she had gotten up out of her chair. Rhoades made an ineffectual grab for her arm saying, "Now don't get in a snit, honey. There's nothing personal in this—it's just business. Christ, you'd think this was the first time you ever heard the phrase 'you scratch my back and I'll scratch yours'!"

"No, it is not, Mr. Rhoades," she replied in an icy manner. "Thank you for reminding me of reality. I'll send you the cost of the meal, it certainly has been worth it." She walked out past the smartly dressed business lunchers, past the frosty maître d', out onto the avenue for the walk home.

Fletcher had done as much as warn her—no, he had frankly and unapologetically defined his character and his motivations to her as far back as that little monologue in his old office. She had blithely ignored the baldest truths, as if they couldn't possibly apply to her. He might be ruthless and cold-blooded, but not with *her.* He might be out to beat the rats at their own game, but that couldn't mean using *her* as a game piece.

Well, it did. Carla Copeland the filmmaker would have shrugged it off. But she had handed him the other Carla, the untried, tender Carla. It was her own fault that she hurt.

When she got back to her studio the numbness that had set in was the only thing that got her through the last messy job needed to cut herself free—calling Fletcher.

Annette's voice on the phone gave her the brief, cowardly hope that she could avoid talking to him in person.

"Carla! Hey, how was lunch with the ferret-face? Fletcher's been bouncing off the walls waiting for you to come back. I'll transfer your call."

Then her fears were realized; the next voice was Fletcher's. "Carla? Where are you?"

She forced herself to be nonchalant. "Oh, I came back to my studio to work."

He sounded unsure. "To work? But..."

"Yeah, you know it occurred to me that I really have a lot of tape, easily enough to do this documentary, so I don't have to lug a camera around behind you anymore."

"That's great, but I thought we had something else in mind for the rest of the day. What's the hurry?"

"Well, Rhoades reminded me this *is* a business, after all. No sense in playing around when I could be fulfilling my contract."

Fletcher became stern; Carla could almost see his dark eyebrows descend in concern. "Carla, what did Rhoades say to you? He must have said something—you're not acting like yourself."

"Why, not at all. We had a perfectly unremarkable conversation about the industry. He just reminded me that I was—*am* in the industry and I'd better act like it. I've enjoyed our time together, Fletcher. I just hope you haven't...umm...taken our fun too much to heart."

There was such a silence on the other end of the phone that Carla was afraid he could hear the raggedness of her breath. When he finally replied his own voice was stiff and forced. "You've caught me a bit off balance...I..."

Not daring to hear what he intended to add, she sallied into a light conclusion. "Well, that's one advantage of being a movie brat, nothing ever surprises me. I've seen it all, every type of behavior known to man, and I never take any of what I see seriously. It's a good working philosophy. And speaking of work, I'm going to sign off and get at it. You'll get a copy of the finished tape to approve. So long."

She hung up shaking.

She knew that eventually the hurt would stop—a body could not sustain it at such a level forever. You either pulled back into balance or you snapped. Carla felt so wretched she hardly cared which happened. On second thought, maybe snapping *would* be better; then she wouldn't have to suffer the humiliating memory of how she had let her feelings creep out from under her guard and tie themselves to Fletcher Arendt—a man *most* unlikely to cherish them. Oh, he had known so well how to lure her! The sweet, civilized ploys of courting had no power over her. She found them as easy to ignore as empty dinner conversation. She had flattered herself that she operated on a deeper level, with concerns of a richer hue and weightier value in the cosmos. So Fletcher had obstructed her, tricked her, tormented her and taken her by storm until she had had nothing to cling to but the sure ground of his charm. He had dived into her stronghold and rocked her very foundations. He had deftly proved to her that right alongside her independence and self-reliance lived a need to lose herself in passion.

Such a profound journey for her, so slight a jaunt for him.... Now she found herself in a wild, threatening territory, no path for miles, no guideposts to look toward.

In the early hours of the next morning, eyes hot and dry, throat a knot of pain from clenching in on itself, Carla looked around at the studio. She had evidently thrown things or perhaps only knocked them over, she couldn't remember. Her hands were clenched in her sheets, and the fabric twined around her legs and wrists like fetters, as oppressive as her sense of being lost. She had to do something to get out of this emotional chaos.

But what did she have to guide her out? She had protected herself so well for so long she knew nothing of how to mend a ruptured heart. She only knew film....

She *did* know film. She had that one guidepost, that one tool, and a hand trained to use it. She had Fletcher Arendt's aggressive, compelling personality on hours and hours of magnetic tape. She had always used video to make sense out of the world; she would use it to make sense out of him.

Chapter Nine

It took a week to cut the documentary, a week in which her hurt sank into a numbed sort of existence, worked its way into the bedrock of her emotions and left her grim. Rage only occasionally surfaced to add its venom to her work; most of the time she was propelled by a gray sense of inevitability. She had learned Fletcher Arendt the hard way, but now she knew him. Every filmmaker, she told herself, whether reporting as a journalist or expressing as an artist, must show truth, must peel away the cozy illusions that padded people's lives, and must reveal some kernel of hard reality—something that every viewer would bite down upon and know, beyond doubt, was there.

Her documentary had a particularly apt subject for this treatment. After all, she had an inside track on the entertainment world. She had been raised in the enchanted land itself and spent years struggling on her own through its hazards. The illusions around show business were as thick as

castle walls. Like a queen on a float, Mercy Riley smiled
and looked lovely for her audience, while beneath the flowers she was driven by some unexamined, powerful force.
Whether her own ambition or Fletcher's drove her, it was a
dynamo. Normal human concerns and qualms were for
normal humans, not people who were stars or who guided
the careers of stars.

Carla unplugged her phone, seeking to escape whatever
attempts Fletcher might make to talk to her. She ignored the
insistent buzzer from the ground-floor door. On her second
day of work it rang so imperatively she had to clamp headphones on her ears and turn up her audio control. Gino, her
landlord, finally roused her by pounding on the door to the
studio itself and swearing in Italian.

She cautiously opened the door, checking to make sure he
was alone.

"Carla! Carla! Have you gone deaf in your ears or something? There's a man downstairs who says he's been calling
you for a hundred years and you don't answer!"

"What does he look like?" she asked, knowing it could
only be Fletcher.

"Big guy, blond. He's got this wild look in his eye—
scared the pants off me, I tell you. That's why I left him
standing outside. But he made me wonder if you were dead
or something. I mean, I haven't heard a squeak out of you
myself."

"I'm not dead. But I *am* sort of hiding from him."

Gino bent closer, interested. "You in some kind of trouble? Is he a bookie or something?"

"No—old boyfriend." She nearly choked on the words.

He nodded sagely. "Ah, no wonder he's such a bull. You
want I should get rid of him?"

"*Please.*"

"Don't worry about it a moment longer. He's history."
So saying, Gino puffed himself up and descended the stairs
doggedly. Carla did not try to find out what he said to
Fletcher; from the fourth floor she couldn't have heard it,
but the doorbells stopped.

She ended up with one of her strongest videos. She was in
no condition to say whether it was any good, but it *was*
effective. It grabbed the viewer from its first fast cuts of
Billy's rehearsal, fueled by his harsh, propulsive rock,
through to the equally jolting end as Fletcher bundled an
exhausted Mercy into a limousine and stole her from her
fans. Every scene, whether active or still, held on to the
tension of imperative, primal music: the incessant drums,
the taut guitar, the urgency of Mercy's voice as it gathered
breath and soared free of her throat.

Fletcher did indeed glow out of the screen, his golden
light was exaggerated by the darkness through which he
always seemed to move, and which drew one down deep
inside his knowing eyes. She hung the whole video around
that significant monologue in which he had revealed himself as well as words could ever do it. But the power came
in her choice of material to illustrate his words, and the cutting that jarred as Fletcher's own personality could jar.

Exhausted at the end, Carla ran the tape one last time. She
could hardly tell what she had anymore. She was too tired:
her mind insisted on playing and replaying tape that she
knew intellectually she hadn't used. Fatalistically, she called
Dietra for a showing.

"My God, you look like you've been through the war!"
was the redhead's heartfelt comment when she showed up.

"Wasn't that in your original plan?" Carla hadn't spoken
for a week, except to mumble instructions to herself—her
voice rattled.

"Huh?" inquired Dietra, not remembering.

"Never mind. Have a beer. It's showtime."

"You know Fletcher and his partner have been leaving messages for me every day asking if I know what you're doing. Haven't they called you?"

"I unplugged my phone."

"I told them you tend to work like that—immerse yourself in the process of creation, or some other garbage. I was making it up as I went along; you never weirded out before."

"How do you know I've weirded out this time?"

Dietra ignored her. "I was so busy I couldn't get away, but I called the manager of the building—Guiseppe?"

"Gino."

"Right—Gino—and he told me he'd hold the phone up so I could hear you swearing away. I figured you must be all right…"

"Thanks for your tender concern."

Dietra frowned suspiciously. "You *have* weirded out. In fact, those messages from Fletcher sound odd, too. What's the matter?"

"You told Rhoades about my mother, didn't you?"

"Oh…"

"Yeah—*oh*. You couldn't have cared less how you got this video on Fletcher, could you? As long as you got it. Well, I hope you enjoy it."

"Enjoyment" patently didn't fit Dietra's reaction when, fifty minutes later, Carla flicked on the lights. The redhead took a compulsive swig of her second beer and her eyes danced nervously over the furniture before they met Carla's. "Umm…" she began. "It's a bit strong. I mean, it's got a very definite viewpoint."

"I remember your saying something about how you expected my video to be unorthodox. If you actually wanted something bland you should have told me a lot sooner."

Dietra had risen and begun to pace. "No, no...This is the type of video that people will remember because it's so...Is Fletcher really that hard?"

Carla willed her face not to move. "My impressions are on that tape."

"Uh-huh." The other woman chewed on her lip, her thoughts so furiously concentrated they could almost be heard grinding inside her head. "It's just that...just that..."

"Just that?"

"Well, I'm worried about legal problems."

"What kind of legal problems? Come on, Dietra, we're getting older and grayer by the minute."

"Okay, like *libel* for one."

"Libel! There isn't one thing in that video that isn't well-documented fact!"

"Maybe, maybe. It's the way you've put it together. He's a lawyer, too, you know. If he decides he doesn't like it he'll *find* a way to sue us."

"That's a technical problem with a technical solution."

Dietra looked up, hopeful. Carla could tell the potential controversy of the video had excited her. Controversy brought celebrity in its wake and Dietra *was* the sponsor of the video. "What's the solution?"

"Fletcher will sign a release."

"He will? He's seen it?"

"No, not yet, but you know it's my practice to give my subject a private viewing so that they can object before a video goes any further."

The fact that Fletcher had not yet seen the video dampened some of Dietra's ebullience, but she allowed herself a guarded optimism. "Okay, if you can get a release from Fletcher, I'll clear the way at Telemusic. It'll be some job though—mark my words. They don't like to step on any big, powerful toes, even if the toes have signed a release." The humor of this touched neither of them. "Maybe I could take a copy of the video with me?"

Carla firmly shook her head. "No, until Fletcher approves it, this is the only copy. Kitchen video policy."

Dietra nodded in resignation.

In the back of the turmoil that passed as her mind, Carla expected Fletcher to denounce the video and insist that she change or scrap it. No one could truly *enjoy* seeing himself portrayed as that cold and calculating, no matter what he professed in words.

She delivered the cassette with a short note and a blank release form to the office, for once blessed with luck—neither Fletcher nor Annette were there. A receptionist, hired to fill the big outer desk and take the drudge work off Annette's shoulders, cast a cool look of unspoken discouragement at Carla the moment she walked in. How quickly they learned—not a week on the job and already she knew she had to drive off the crackpots who barged through those oak doors. When Carla introduced herself the young woman's manner changed radically and she smiled. For some the smile, for some the rebuff. Carla sighed, handed her the tape and went home to wait. That, too, had a leaden familiarity to it.

Different this time was the speed of Fletcher's response. That very evening, before Carla had time to shake off the attack of nerves that had accompanied her to Arendt/Harrow, a phone call came through her newly replugged-in phone. It was the secretary, working overtime.

"Mr. Arendt is through with the video, Ms. Copeland. He says he'll have a message for you when you come and pick it up."

"Very well, then I'll come by the office..."

"Oh, no, it's not here. He gave me an address for you."
She read off the building number and the street—Fletcher's
home.

Carla nearly gagged. "When did he say I could get it?"

"He said he'd be there all evening."

"Fine. Thank you." She hung up.

She must have known there'd be a final confrontation with
him, although she hadn't allowed herself to imagine that it
might transpire on his home ground—where she had come
so close to losing herself to him irretrievably. Where would
she find the emotional resources to face him again? She felt
so wrung out and drained she feared she would come apart
in pieces before him.

Still unsure how she would handle herself, but driven by
a strange fatalism, Carla set off for Central Park West. The
building at dusk seemed much more ominous than grand.
The ivy in the courtyard made secretive noises in the wind,
like people whispering behind her back. The night doorman was a thin, saturnine man who called up to Fletcher's
apartment in what Carla imagined irrationally to be a disapproving voice.

The door from his private landing stood open again. She
faltered as memory smote her of the first and only time she
had ever walked through that foyer. Gritting her teeth, she
forced herself into the doorway and looked apprehensively
into the vast, darkened living room. The dark shapes of the
sparse furnishings wove through the shadows at the edges
of her vision, but her focus was drawn to the one soft patch
of light that glowed on the group of couches. Fletcher
perched on the back of one sofa and, to Carla's strained per-
ception, the light seemed to come as much from him as from
the low, paper-shaded lamps. Smoke from a cigarette drifted
acridly past his immobile head and she thought, uselessly,
how she hated to see him smoke.

Expressionless, he said, "Well, come in."

There was no help for it—she dredged up one moment's boldness and stepped forward. "Your receptionist said you were done with the video."

He sighed, his movement stirring the smoke into sinuous eddies, and slid onto his feet with the lion-like grace Carla had always found so striking. In a simple white shirt and old jeans his innate strength and beauty worked to their best advantage.

She felt a treacherous weakness in her legs that wasn't just fear. She desperately wanted a glimpse of the flint-hard, fighting Fletcher—the one she had cast in the video. That was the only Fletcher she was prepared to deal with.

"Well, *here*. Take it."

She realized he had produced the cassette and held it out to her while she faltered in confusion. She reached her hand for the plastic case, touched it and nearly dropped it when he abruptly let go. His observant frown warned her that the oddness of her own response was all too obvious. She cleared her throat. "Will there be any legal problems about releasing this to Telemusic?"

"That depends."

"On what?"

"Is this how you really see me?"

She looked at the floor as she spoke. "What kind of a question is that, Fletcher? Weren't you the one always pushing 'the artist's unique vision' business on me? I thought you didn't want a straight documentary from me."

"No, I didn't—not from you. I wanted *your* artist's vision."

"Well, then?"

"I just want to make sure that's what I got. I want to hear it from your own lips."

At his low, fervent tone she looked up and was sorry she had. His eyes glowed like sapphires in the black rock of a mine. Half his face was light and half unnerving shadow, and tension vibrated from him like a current. "Yes, Fletcher," she forced the words through a stiff jaw. "That video is a sincere response to the part of my life I spent in your company."

His eyes bored into hers a second longer, then he pulled a sheet of paper from an envelope beside him and somberly offered it to her—the release. "Then there will be no legal problems."

"Thank you." The feel of the crisp paper in her hand should have been her signal to leave. She stayed, drugged by an ambivalence she didn't understand.

Fletcher's watchful calm finally broke. "For God's sake, Carla, decide what you want. I know I made every mistake in the book with you, but I never thought you were stupid. You have my legal release, do you expect me to give you my blessing?"

"No...I..."

"You *what*? You seem to think I'm exceptionally cold-blooded and insensitive. Well, I'm doing my best to be that for you so you can walk out that door and show your video in good conscience. But if you stay another minute I'm going to tell you just how angry I *am*. Will that be any easier for you? Is anger the one emotion you know how to defend yourself against? I wish you'd teach *me*."

Carla felt tears sting her eyelids. To retaliate she found one last scrap of acting talent. "I think you miss the point, Fletcher. You seem to think I have some indelible emotional investment in how you take this, that I'm waiting for you to give me permission to do my work, to make me valid as a filmmaker. Allow me to take that from your already over-burdened shoulders. I do not rise and fall on the whim of

Fletcher Arendt, no matter how much you may have enjoyed provoking weird reactions in me.

"I have put up with more difficult behavior than yours in order to make other videos. Don't think you presented me with the ultimate challenge or that I ever lost sight of the reason I was here. My work always comes first and anything else is a *distant* second. We came to the understanding long ago that everyone has his own motivations, so any *mis*understandings were on your side."

"I see," he said softly, staring at her from the darkness. "It was romantic of me to see you as a whole human being then, wasn't it? As a woman who might be touched?"

Carla's face burned. She forced herself to reply coolly, "I know you're not used to making that kind of mistake."

"No, I'm not. Thank you for being so frank. Now you'd better leave or I may make a few more mistakes."

Alarm moved her, alarm and something hot and miserable that made her want to escape the look in his eyes, for it was hurt, not anger, that stared at her so accusingly. Clutching the video and the crumpled release, she turned on a trembling foot and fled into the waiting elevator.

Fletcher sank down into the nest of couch pillows. His muscles seemed to have suddenly turned to pudding and his nerve endings to ice. He wouldn't have noticed if he had sat down on nails. Severe dislocation spun his brain in a sickening whirl. He couldn't believe what had just happened. He had always sensed that dealing with Carla was something akin to juggling fire, but he had also always assumed, without weighing the case, that she *would* come around. He had seen hints of it so many times, and he felt so much of himself in her—his own stubborn pride, his own need to strive and work, his sensitivity and his corresponding temper—that he had made the ultimate mistake of seeing her *as* himself. How well could one human being know another, especially when blinded by hope?

She *wasn't* him. She had taken that video with every intention of releasing it. Her ''sincere response'' to the part of her life she had spent in his company, she had called it— venom and vitriol. Despite her brave nonsense about having endured him for the sake of her work, he didn't believe for a moment that her warm responses had been faked. He had touched something in her, all right, he knew *that* as surely as he knew that she had touched him. But then it had all fallen apart. She had learned to respond to him before she had learned to trust him. Thus she was only too ready to hide her heart behind the absurd belief that he had intended to use her. As if it made any difference to him that she was related to Amelia Abbott-Copeland! She might have been related to half the crowned heads of Hollywood and he couldn't have wanted her any more. She might have been related to *no one* and he couldn't have loved her any less. But there was no way to prove this to her. He had lost his gamble. He had played with fire and been scorched.

Carla spent another sleepless night. Immediately after leaving Fletcher's apartment she had felt dazed, but very quickly her wits had returned and administered a solid slap to her conscience. It was as if a madness had been lifted from her. As often as she had accused Fletcher of driving her into nosense, she realized that she had managed it sublimely on her own. With nothing but confusion and wounded pride she had created a version of Fletcher so thoroughly inhuman it made no sense that she could have fallen in love with him. And she had convinced herself day after day, night after night, in front of her video monitors, that he really *was* this monster.

Some journalist...Some documentary. Had she actually intended this vicious portrayal to be seen by the world? Or had she just wanted to take a stab at Fletcher for rocking her own self-image? Perhaps she had subconsciously expected him to rant and rave and threaten, to act just like the ogre she had made him out to be. Then she could have felt righteous indignation. It would have been very neat, very easy.

But he had handed her a release. If he had signed that release in *blood* she still could not have turned in her video. She knew this beyond the shadow of a doubt. So where was she now? She had a video that she would shortly erase from start to finish, she had hours and hours of raw tape that she simply couldn't bear to look at again. For the first time in her life, she was going to have to break a contract.

"What do you mean, you're not handing over the video?" Dietra's voice showed a greater than usual degree of seriousness.

"It's not a hard concept, Dietra. I'm not handing over the video, not any of it—not my notes or rough tape, nothing. I'm defaulting on my contract. It can't be the first time this has ever happened to Telemusic. I'll give them the name of my lawyer and they can thrash it out."

"Well, it's the first time it's ever happened to *me*! I thought you were my *friend*. How can you do this?"

Carla held the phone away from her face, hoping Dietra might not hear the gnashing of her teeth. The impulse to retaliate was almost too strong to resist—but she fought it warily now. If she brought up the little matter of Dietra's own betrayal, she'd have to explain exactly how it had affected her relationship with Fletcher and she could do without Dietra knowing that.

"Look, Dietra, this is not a personal plot for your destruction, but neither is it open to negotiation. I've already returned the advance money. Telemusic can sue for damages or we can settle for something out of court..."

"He wouldn't sign that release, would he?"

"Actually, he *did* sign it."

"Then why..."

"Because I no longer think I have a worthwhile contribution to make to this project and I want *out*. End of discussion."

Dietra made several disgruntled sounds, but before she could gather her breath for a full-fledged assault, Carla bade her good-bye and hung up.

Now that she could leave her studio without fear of running into an irate Fletcher, Carla found she lacked the energy. She lay in bed or dragged around listlessly reading out-of-date film magazines and having her food sent up from the corner deli.

Word evidently had not spread to all corners of the universe that she had broken her contract with Telemusic because three more proposals came in her mail even as she had preliminary talks with her lawyer. The proposals sat unopened on her worktable. She was burned out, bleached of energy; she couldn't have picked up a camera to save it from being run over by a car. She needed a change in her life and a vacation was the only thing that came to mind. With a bit more vigor than she had shown in days, she made airline reservations to Los Angeles.

Chapter Ten

Fletcher leaned against the windowsill, stared out at the light-spangled lake twenty floors below, and realized he didn't know what city he was in...ah, Detroit. Was that a Great Lake out there? Huron? Erie? No time to find out—they moved on tomorrow to Chicago—and really no point. Billy's tour was going well. He pulled enormous, ecstatic crowds in the rock 'n' roll crazy Midwest. Annette reported that Mercy adored Canada, and the novelty of playing new cities like Montreal and Quebec had quite offset her pique at touring without Fletcher.

He had always known she would come around. Their interests had been diverging for years. Mercy craved glamour and stardom, movie roles, jet-set friends. Fletcher loved the rough, early years of carting the amplifiers in station wagons, gluing up tour posters himself, the incomparable thrill of hearing his band on the radio for the first time.

Billy, too, would be over the top soon; the time of struggling in garages was just about over for him. Fletcher could handle two artists at a time without slighting either. Now that Annette had Mercy, he could begin to scout seriously for his next project.

In nearly every city he managed to get to a club or two, to chat with local disc jockeys and record store managers, even kids on the street. But nothing excited him. He heard and recognized talent, made phone calls to friends at record companies on behalf of occasional youngsters, but he found no one in whom he wanted to invest his own life. It was as if he had lost the little spark that always flared when talent came his way.

He had thought at first that he had lost his romantic idealism because of Carla. He had sensed such love and life and excitement in her, bottled up by that iron will of hers, but sparkling all the same. He had been *sure* he could free it just by the force of his love. When she had left his apartment that day, fully intending to release the video, he thought the last of his idiotic romantic notions had been killed by her malice.

And then she hadn't released it. Rhoades, purple with rage, called Fletcher in Philadelphia to demand that he *make* Carla keep to her contract—as if Fletcher had any influence. But, even though he knew his faith had not been totally misplaced, his spirits refused to rise. It was all he could do to plunge himself into the details of Billy's tour. He was tired, more tired than he could ever remember.

"You going to lie around that pool for the rest of your life?" Amelia Abbott-Copeland's voice rang out clear as crystal through the huge enclosed patio—the voice that had taken famous directors to task and quelled the tantrums of stars for twenty years. It had no effect on her daughter.

"I'm not tanned yet," Carla replied.

"You're not *going* to tan—you're a strawberry blonde. You're just going to burn and peel and burn and peel until all your lily white skin comes *off*."

"Aw, come on, Mother! What good is it to have a big house in Southern California if not so your poor pale daughter can come visit you and turn into a Frito?"

Her mother replied ambiguously, "I can't argue with logic like that."

Carla listened for further murmurs from her parent, heard none and tried to slink back into her sun-baked coma. She failed. Her mother's words had roused something in her, some restlessness that now flicked its tail back and forth like an irritable cat. Why couldn't she just cook her brains out in peace? She hadn't given herself a vacation since graduating from film school four long, hard years ago.

She stared around at the green-tiled pool. Its color and shape made it look like a huge lily pad in the midst of a plant-hung jungle—her father's doing. He had created a lush oasis in the heat-cracked ravines of Mesquite Canyon. The interior of the house was as cool and comfortable as the patio, all pure, Oriental proportions and eye-soothing stretches of space. It was different in detail from Fletcher's penthouse, but Fletcher would have liked it.

With a disgruntled curse, Carla sat up. Her restlessness thrashed freely now. For hours on end, sometimes even a whole day or two at a time, she had been able to keep that inflaming name out of her mind. But each time it made contact with the edges of her consciousness, it burned her. Fletcher Arendt. He was the *past*. She had made a bad mistake, corrected it as much as humanly possible and now she meant to get on with the rest of her life. But he was so tenacious! He was like a singe mark in a tabletop—you could keep arranging the placemats to cover it, but every time you cleared the table—there it was.

He'd like that analogy....

Why couldn't he have been a raging, blustering jerk about the blasted video? Really, she felt she merited at least a few veiled threats, if not an outright attempt on her life. What had he given her instead? Eyes full of wounded hope and some soft line about having thought she was a woman who might be touched.

He *had* touched her—that was one hundred percent of the problem. She had struggled and fought her own common sense, her own sense of self-preservation in order to lay her heart at his feet, and she had found out his whole behavior toward her had been a pretense from beginning to end. So much for trust.

Her thoughts went round, day after day, no matter how she tried to distract herself with mindless errands and sight-seeing. Her mother spent busy hours on the phone, pursuing the legal and artistic arrangements for her new film. Her father came home every evening from his dental office smelling of grape fluoride and silver amalgam, puttered with his African violets and never made a comment. Yet Carla felt the atmosphere gathering into a black thunder-cloud above her sunburned head.

The constant calls from her lawyer in New York helped keep the whole brew in constant tumult. The woman was too conscientious. Carla just wanted the case settled.

"Really, I think we could hold out for a lower settlement."

"No, Ms. Mann, I don't care how much they want—I mean within reason—I just want it to be done with."

"But look at the precedents—this happens all the time. You didn't even throw them off schedule because your segment wasn't planned to be shown until *next year*! They've got time to commission half a *dozen* replacement videos!"

"Ms. Mann, I don't care! Just decide on a figure so I can start planning on how I'm going to pay it!"

Argh! In many ways it did Carla good to hear how small a ripple she had created in the corporate domain of Telemusic. It gave her some perspective. Dietra would not lose her job, no matter how melodramatically she tore her red hair. The rock fans of the universe would not know what they were missing because Fletcher, no matter how influential, was part of the *hidden* world of rock. This fiasco wouldn't even make much of a bruise on her own career; one soured project in four years of above-average success would horrify no one. Already Gino had forwarded mail to her containing two new proposals for documentary work.

So it seemed she had gotten off scot-free. Or she would have, were it not for this intermittent knifing sensation in her heart. How in the world had her parents gotten together and stayed contentedly married through all the years of her mother's flashy success? Her father had been a quiet dental student when they had met, she an aggressive director's assistant. The circumstance that threw them together had been an utterly unremarkable blind date—no drama, no deep mutual suspicion, no competition or anxiety over the other's motives. At least none they ever spoke of later. She had always accepted her parents' marriage as one of the unquestionable facts of life—like rocks or trees or air travel. Now she found herself amazed that people could manage to marry at all. What did it take? Her father was as placid as a dog by the fire, enjoying the heat of his wife's ambition. But did he ever feel jealous or outshone?

"I would have been a pretty rotten dentist if I had tried to use it as a route to glory, honey," he observed to his daughter one evening after dinner. Carla had wandered into his fern-filled study, where he retired frequently to study his professional journals and plant catalogs. He had given up pipes because smoke made his plants ill, and now contented himself with mugs of fragrant herb tea. Carla wondered how she had sprung from someone so mild and well-adjusted.

He continued with an understanding smile on his round face. "I get satisfaction from the work itself. I *know* it's worthwhile. I don't need flatterers to tell me so."

"I know, Daddy. I got *that* from you, at least, and from Mother, too. I just sometimes wish I had picked work that was less potentially fashionable, then I could concentrate on *it* and not worry about the other stuff."

"It's all in your attitude. Here I am giving a parent lecture..."

"No, no! Go on! Any advice you can give me is more than I can give myself."

"All right. You can get distracted by silly stuff in any field. It's up to *you* to keep your mind clear and focused. I know you think I've been hibernating like a honey bear in my office all these years, but it hasn't always been so. It sounds ludicrous, but patients used to come to me because I was married to your mother."

"To get their teeth fixed?"

"Sure. They'd come in to get caps or braces for that perfect smile and make very certain to tell me how talented they were and how eager they'd be to work in a high-quality production like one of Amelia's. Of course all this was hard to say with a mouthful of gauze and steel mirrors, but they always made their point."

"You must have felt a little annoyed that they'd chosen you for that rather than your actual skill."

"No," he chuckled. "I fixed them, all right—I gave them good care. I never got them into Amelia's movies, but they ended up becoming regular patients anyway."

Carla grinned wryly. "Okay, I get the moral—press on regardless and to thine own self be true."

"Lord, did I come off so stuffy?"

"That's what parents are for."

"I'm kidnapping you," Amelia announced one day, throwing a bright hat over her gray-streaked coppery hair.

"Oh, yeah?" Carla looked up from her book, curious.

"Yeah. Go hop in the car. Actually I've got to return a couple of computer discs to the Martins and that long drive just bores me to tears."

"Gerry and Valerie Martin?"

"Oh, you *do* remember them!" her mother exclaimed melodramatically. "Yes, the very same Gerry and Valerie Martin whom you refuse to go see or even call when they get out to New York, even though they used to be like family to you…"

"Oh, Mother, you know Gerry would just try to give me a job on one of his films."

"God forbid he should do you any favors."

"That's exactly it. He *would* just be trying to do me a favor."

"I suppose so. He certainly wouldn't be getting anything back for himself, employing a talentless, inexperienced, useless…"

Carla sighed exaggeratedly and her mother let the sentence drift off. They slid onto the baked seats of the car in silence, but, as she started the engine, her mother inquired levelly, "So, are we keeping to the story that you're just bumming around New York working odd jobs, or what? They *know* you went to film school."

"Oh, I don't know…" Carla replied in exasperation. "Maybe it'd be better if I just stayed home…"

But her mother made short work of that suggestion by squealing out of the driveway and onto the dusty canyon road. Carla slumped into the leather seat letting the dry, hot wind whip her face, knowing she had just let herself be roped into something significant. She knew her mother was tired of going along with her secret life as a filmmaker; she wanted to boast of a bright, accomplished daughter. Carla was tired of it, too. The charade had taken too much of her creative energy over the years. The incident—could she refer to it so blithely?—with Fletcher had forced her to see how wearying such a tangle could become. She had spent the past several years looking over her shoulder anxiously and allowing suspicion to shape her feelings for other people. She had always done this in order to protect what she called the "real Carla". But, thus protected, what had *happened* to the real Carla? Had she become an unbalanced, crazily erratic fugitive rather than the warm, feeling soul of a whole person?

The canyon walls zipped by—sunny culverts cracked by the recent drought, flashes of pink and white stucco as estates sparkled into and out of view, the brittle mesquite and unearthly looking century plants. Did this look at all like Fletcher's home in New Mexico? She stiffened at the thought.

Without warning, they reached the rough pine gateposts and cattle guard of the Martin's ranch. The car jounced across the pipes laid to deter the more adventurous cattle and followed the winding drive to the sprawling main house. The Martins ran enough horses and cattle to require a small staff of ranch hands. It gave their place a pleasantly down-to-earth character.

Valerie Martin, a film editor in her own right, had set up a complete editing lab in one wing of the great house. She regularly edited the movies her husband produced, but in between found herself in hot demand by the rest of the industry. Carla vividly remembered being taught to run a Moviola before her twelfth birthday. Her whole movie fas-

cination had started at least that early, happily fostered by
these close friends.

"My God, it's the thin, sunburned ghost of a little girl I
used to know!" Valerie yelled across the central courtyard.
She came jogging over the flagstones, past white iron furniture, trailing long trims of movie film. She tended to
squint from both the brilliant desert sun and the hours of
close work in her studio, and it gave her an angry, critical
expression that did not reflect her sweet nature.

"Why, you're the very image of Carla Abbott-Copeland,
who went to New York and then dropped off the face of the
earth." Valerie stopped with her hands on her hips and
peered through wire-rimmed glasses. "But thin! That lobs-
ter-pink color makeup you're wearing is not flattering,
child."

"Guess I'm overdoing the vacation bit a little," Carla
grinned, happy to be back in range of this woman's teasing.
"I'm hoping to look healthy when I go back east."

"I think you're doing something wrong. Never mind,
come in! Hi, Amelia! Didn't mean to ignore you. I'll yell for
Gerry. We've been losing hair over this picture the last few
weeks. He'll be tickled to see Carla and have something else
to think about for a while. Ger!"

She led them through room after room of cool, glossy
blue-and-white tile and white-washed stucco, and settled
them in the messy room outside the editing lab. "He won't
go more than twenty feet away from his baby," Valerie con-
fided. "He thinks the film will self-destruct or something.
I *wish*."

Carla caught a glimpse of long, cluttered worktables and
big green Moviola machines that made her mouth water.
Three weeks away from work and she was suffering
withdrawal.

Amelia sank comfortably into a chaise. "How's it going?"

Valerie rolled her eyes. "Well, only an act of God is going to see us anywhere near the December release date. Gerry's been holding off the backers with a lot of assurances, but the fact is we're absolutely swamped. John Kramer, this boy genius director Gerry was so enthralled with, *is* talented, I'll freely admit, but without the sense of a sunstruck iguana. We need about twenty-five minutes of really snappy, tense action footage and this kid, intent on covering every camera angle, every combination of tricks known to man, had handed in ten hours of film. And almost none of it is properly annotated or organized. Just reels and reels of film. Gerry and I have each aged a decade."

"No assistants?" Amelia inquired.

Valerie sat and propped her espadrille-shod feet on a chest of brass and tooled leather. "Oh, they come and go. You know how hard it is to find a really sharp kid these days who's willing to slog through the junk work. Actually, what we need is another *editor*. This is the first time I've ever felt out of my depth with a film. Frankly, I don't know if we even have a film right now. I've been running on four hours of sleep a night for two weeks and I can't even remember what the darn picture is about. Horse racing, I think. Oh, listen to me bending your ear with this nonsense! After I raved about your being such a welcome distraction! Why, look who's rising from the dead—guess who's here, Gerry!"

A pudgy, bleary-faced man emerged from the studio and sagged against the doorframe. "I have just watched that stuntman fall off his horse three hundred and seventy-eight times. I feel awful."

Despite the complaints and groans from each half of this team, Carla sensed their deeper absorption in the film process, bogged down though they might now be. Several times she had opened her mouth to commiserate with a story of similar desperation or to ask technical questions, and each time she had barely stopped herself. The Martin's film contacts were so extensive that telling them would be equivalent to telling the whole industry. So she held her tongue, but felt her pulse trip in unexpected envy.

Unhindered by such concerns, her mother dove right into the discussion. The more Carla heard, the more she itched to contribute. By the time they left the ranch her head whirred with ideas, her body throbbed with restlessness. She *must* start work again!

Her mother shrewdly said nothing, limiting herself to a few surreptitious looks in her daughter's direction, but Carla caught them. "All *right,* Mother," she groaned. "Very neatly done. Now I'm miserable and dying to get back to New York."

"I never intended to chase you out—why don't you find some little thing you could do around here?"

"You mean like help Valerie edit?"

"Why not? You edit your own videos; you know the craft, even if it isn't your main interest. They need an experienced assistant who's familiar with the way they work. You can't have forgotten everything you learned from hanging out with them all those afternoons after school."

"No, but..."

"But what? Don't give me any of this folderol about not wanting to accept favors, Carla."

"Hmm...I guess I was going to say something like that."

"But on second thought, maybe you're going to be reasonable?"

"*Maybe,*" Carla said severely. Then she cracked a smile. "But I also reserve the right to be *un*reasonable."

There was silence for a few minutes, then Amelia resumed in a soft, serious tone. "You know, I've always been very flattered at how you've tried to be like me, Carla.''

Carla looked at her mother in surprise. ''You noticed?''

''Of course I noticed. I never would have wanted to make it on the basis of my name either. But there are two major differences between us.''

''What?''

''I never *had* a name till I made it for myself, of course. I had a whole different set of problems than you. I'm not saying you *should* throw your name around or that your problems are any less difficult than mine were. I'm saying they're *different*. You can't solve them using my methods.''

Carla murmured indistinctly, then asked, ''What's the second difference?''

''You're an artist.''

''And you're not?''

''And I'm not.''

''Mother!''

''No, really. I'm not putting myself down—I'm a sensational businesswoman, I'm a good general, a fair psychologist and an astute judge of talent. Thus I am a good producer. But I am *not* an artist. You are. Your father and I always wondered where you came by your genes. Neither of us has the slightest idea what it's like to be creative so we've never been able to help you learn to fit into your own skin, but we've always believed you'd be able to figure it out for yourself.''

''Until now?''

''We *still* believe it. We just feel a little helpless sometimes, watching you work so hard *against* yourself. I mean these endless documentaries, for instance...I know you're bored as sure as I know by the look on your father's face when one of his plants has died.''

Carla grumbled miserably, ''This sounds familiar.''

"Oh? Someone else has been giving you sage advice?"

"Yeah."

"Was he or she as brilliant, capable and shrewd as your mother?"

"Yes, he was."

"Then I'll shut up."

Though her mother *did* spare her any more lectures or "sage advice," Carla's mind wouldn't let the subject lie. What was she going to do with the rest of her life? Fletcher, damn him, had ensured one thing—she could never again go back to sleepwalking through documentaries. Whatever he had awakened in her personally had filtered through her entire being and left her changed. Her own mother had finally broken years of silence to tell her she had made a major error somewhere in the course of trying to grow up.

As if to irritate herself into making some sort of decision, Carla turned on the television that night, flipping through the cable stations in search of the west coast's version of Telemusic. She found it: rock videos, rock interviews, album news, contests to meet the stars, outrageously dressed announcers who all bore a generic resemblance to Dietra. Calling herself a perverse, self-destructive idiot, Carla watched two hours of glossily produced, violent, sexist videos, with one or two good ones thrown in accidentally, until the tour news came on.

Mercy Riley, with her audience older than the typical rock-cable subscriber, was not mentioned, but Billy Pilgrim, the rising star, was their featured story. His tour had so far taken him through the east coast and now advanced into the rock 'n' roll heartlands—Detroit, Chicago, Milwaukee. Everywhere he had enjoyed sellout crowds, heavy press, booming album sales. The station ran clips of him signing records at a big store in Madison, Wisconsin, his ecstatic smile almost too big for his thin face to hold.

Carla found herself searching involuntarily for a glimpse of shining blond hair on the fringes of the blue-jeaned crowd. She found none. Fletcher performed his magic well in the background, but Carla now saw his hand in everything from the dramatic store displays to the carefully offhand manner in which Billy responded to interview questions. It suddenly struck her that though she was not like her mother, Fletcher was. The job of manager was as vast and indefinable as that of producer. They did anything and everything; they devised huge, all-encompassing plans, they just as willingly wrapped tape around electrical cords. Their personalities were similar, too, Fletcher's and her mother's. Both combined indomitable wills with a fine sensitivity to other people's feelings. That balance was necessary for true success. A more ruthless person might achieve glory for himself, but Carla had finally made herself admit that this was not Fletcher's desire. She had made many serious mistakes in the past. It was time to start correcting them.

The next morning, before the sun had warmed the lizards to life on the patio, Carla set off through the canyons in her parents' spare car. She felt reborn, vigorous, hopeful. Sometime in the night a decision had percolated up from her subconscious and when she woke she found it in full bloom, like a pot of flowers, in the front of her mind.

The Martins' ranch looked, if possible, even brighter and busier than before. Gerry flashed by on a white Arabian horse, the very picture of a weekend cowboy. This was how a famous producer dealt with a film in trouble? Carla had to wait for the explanation until she found Valerie in the cutting room.

"You know, I just saw your husband thundering up into the hills on a horse."

Valerie looked up wearily from the viewer of a Moviola. "Did he have any saddlebags?"

"Uh, no...I don't think so."

"Good, then he's not *escaping*." She giggled girlishly and motioned for Carla to clear a seat for herself on one of the cluttered stools. "Actually, I sent him out to have a little fun. The pressure is beginning to make him turn colors—mainly red and gray."

"It's not going too well?"

"Honestly, Carla, I can't tell. It's like I told you yesterday—we've been so close to it for so long we can't see what we're doing anymore."

"Would a fresh eye help?"

"Sure would. Wait, you mean yours?"

The moment had come. Carla took a deep, bracing breath and said, "I guess I've never told you what I've been doing in New York all these years."

Valerie frowned and looked away, oddly flustered. "Uh, no..."

"I finished film school and have run a video production company for four years. I get a lot of work."

Valerie's reaction was strange. "Thank God!" she exclaimed. "Now I don't have to pretend to be blind, deaf and dumb anymore!"

"Huh?"

"Oh, honey, we've known about your work, but your mother made us swear the most awful vows of silence you can imagine; we couldn't mention it to you or hire you on for jobs or give your name to anyone we knew...It was awful! I hope you're not mad. We couldn't help knowing, and we did *try*."

Carla sat shaking her head, a self-deprecating smile on her face. Of course her mother couldn't have kept it from her closest friends. She remembered so many awkward occasions when she had come home for a visit and run into Gerry or Valerie, how they had never pressured her for information on what she was up to in New York. She had thought they weren't particularly interested...

"No, it's okay, Valerie. Thank you for letting me try things my way for so long."

"What made you change your mind?"

Carla stared up at her frankly. "A man."

"Ah. A man you don't want to talk about?"

"Right."

"Well, I know you're as silent as the grave when you want to be, so I'm not even going to ask. Tell me, are you any good as a film editor?"

"Damn good."

"Okay, take these reels and give me seven seconds of a guy falling off his horse—snappy, exciting, a little off-beat."

"Is this the same guy who was falling off his horse yesterday?"

Valerie buried her red-eyed face in her hands and groaned, "Yes, and if you can't cut this for me I'm going to go out and throw myself under Gerry's horse!"

Carla spent a good part of the morning rummaging through the endless versions of the fall—there was simply too much film. Valerie was right; this whole project needed a fresh eye. She sat back and let a sequence fall into place on her mind's own movie screen—quick, concise, exciting. She had always had a strong sense of rhythm and timing, an almost musical eye. The biggest problem was searching through the miles of film for the frames that matched the version she had in her head.

Valerie and Gerry critiqued her tiny contribution to their production over a lunch of cheese sandwiches and iced tea. Gerry smelled faintly horsey, but seemed much less high-strung than he had a day earlier. He ran the film again, turned to his wife, eyes damp with relief, and then said to Carla, "As of this morning you're on the payroll...I mean, if you're willing to jump onto a sinking ship."

"I can't imagine any ship of yours sinking, Gerry."

"This one will unless we dump some more of this useless film. You seem to be good at it. Do you want the job?"

Before Carla could answer, Valerie nudged him and looked stern. "What about credits?"

"Oh, yeah. Oh, it goes without saying you'll have full credit as an editor. I never try to hide good work." He peered curiously back at his wife, a little hurt. "Has anyone been telling this child that I'd try to take credit for her work or something?"

Carla knew what Valerie had meant to do and she hastened to soothe Gerry. "No, Gerry, nothing like that. Valerie just wants me to know I'm getting into the big time."

"Well, yes, I guess you are. It'll open doors for you, even in New York, if I do say so myself. Why are you two laughing?"

Chapter Eleven

Eager as Carla felt to dive into the cutting of the film, Valerie and Gerry sternly forced her to drive into L.A. the next day and join the local branch of the film editors' union. Only then did they hand her the fat script book and a grease pencil and let her go to work.

The film, entitled *The Pacesetter*, was indeed an enormous mess. Carla spent a week watching the first cut and skimming through the thirty hours of extra raw film. Her own videos had been wonderfully economical in comparison with this lavish production. Five film barrels sat across one wall, long tendrils of celluloid hanging into them from a pipe hung across the ceiling. The first cut itself was three hours long, filled with awkward transitions, gaping holes and dead scenes. Valerie admitted freely that they hadn't managed to get a grip on the problem yet and Gerry was due in Florida to start shooting a new picture in a month.

Carla dug in. She arrived at eight o'clock every morning armed with notes on things that had occurred to her the previous night. She made Valerie hire two filmmaking students to wind film, code spools and keep meticulous notes in the script book. Valerie, to whom all this was old hat, chuckled good-naturedly at Carla's authoritarian manner and started calling her "The Doctor," but she listened with great attention to her new coeditor's advice.

The new movements of editing soon became second nature to Carla. With one white-gloved hand she would loosely hold the strip of film as it spun through the editing machine; an assistant's voice would say from the speakers "Scene twenty-one, take seven"; a prop man would set a door slamming on the set; an actress would say her line. Stop the film, mark the frame with grease pencil, fly through the next stretch of unusable film, mark another frame. The actress would speak her second line. Stop, cut, splice the two segments together with tape, hang the deleted trim from a pin in the wall in front of her, bend back to the Moviola.

The assistants busily fetched film, rewound the ever-tangled skeins that sprawled across the floor, organized their lists of frame counts. Carla grew so used to the sound of film being run backward over tape heads that she sometimes imagined she could understand what was being said.

Her back ached, her eyes went into spasms, she dreamed in fast cuts and slow fades, but she *loved* the work. The best bonus of all was that she had no time to think about Fletcher.

By the time Gerry left for Florida they were able to show him a second cut that approximated a well-paced, stylish film. He boarded the plane wearing a relaxed smile, no longer morbidly worried that they wouldn't make their Christmas release. Then they got down to the nitty-gritty work of refining every scene, foot by foot, frame by frame.

Seven weeks later they sent the completed film to the sound studio and four weary but elated film editors drove to Valerie's favorite restaurant, had a scrumptious dinner—charged to the film studio—and got marvellously sloshed on champagne.

"Oh, it's really a shame that film editors get no glory," Valerie moaned fervently. "They'd build monuments to us…"

"Yeah, but as tired as I feel, they'd be memorials to a dead person," Carla replied, almost limp with exhaustion.

Jane, one of the assistants, groaned in agreement, and then protested, "But, Valerie, you've got no cause to complain—Gerry is one of the few producers who ever acknowledges his editor."

"He has to, the egomanical cur—in case you haven't noticed, I'm *married* to him. But all you guys are going to get is credits. Oh, and an invite to the premiere of your choice. What'll it be, Carla? West coast or east coast?"

"East coast. I'm going back to New York."

"I figured. Too bad though—I could hang Gerry on your arm and you'd get a little press attention at least."

Carla shook her head amiably. "It's okay, Val. You know I'm not a glory-seeker."

"Hey, I thought you turned over a new leaf, using your new name and all."

"I'm just admitting it, I'm not *bargaining* with it." In order to save the conversation from even this slip into seriousness, she joked, "If I wanted media attention I wouldn't have gotten involved with lowlifes like film editors."

The two youngsters, as Valerie benevolently called the assistants, staggered out of the restaurant at eleven o'clock, leaving their "elders" to order another round of cordials and eye the dessert menu.

"Oh hell, Carla, I've been denying myself all evening out of habit. I'm having the baklava. I'm having *two* of the baklavas."

"Me, too." Carla had slouched so far back into the puffy chair she didn't know if she could lean forward to eat any baklava. She had gotten drunk so few times in her life, always having the excuse of work to take her home early, that the snug, misty feeling had taken her by surprise.

"So," Valerie exclaimed after her first blissful bite of pastry. "Will your studio still be standing when you get back to New York?"

"I suppose so. My landlord sent me mail only a few days ago, so the wall with the mailboxes on it must still be there."

"How goes the infamous Telemusic affair?"

"Grinding to a boring close. Dietra doesn't even razz me about it anymore. It seems she found another filmmaker to replace me and she's half-engaged to him, so she's less inclined to view me as the villain of the story now."

"Ah, the filter of love..."

An involuntary groan escaped Carla's throat. Valerie looked up shrewdly. "You ever going to tell me about the man who changed your mind?"

"No."

"Just thought maybe enough time had passed for...well, for whatever. But it's none of my business. Have another cognac. Waiter!"

Her studio did indeed still stand when Carla stepped out of the taxi a few days later. Gino stopped hosing the sidewalk long enough to give her a bear hug and start haranguing her immediately thereafter. "Hey, it's lonely without you up there! I keep missing the sound of you dropping things and swearing. You back for good?"

"Yep," she replied brightly. "For good or for bad, until the next time I leave."

Gino frowned. "Sounds like the runaround. You learn to talk like that in L.A.?"

She laughed and hiked upstairs. At the sight of all her dust-covered equipment, so many contradictory feelings came back to her that she halted halfway across the floor, short of breath. It was like walking right back into the middle of the wretched day she had left New York thirteen weeks ago. The film magazines that had failed to distract her lay scattered in the same heaps, envelopes of proposals covered her worktable, her bed still looked as if it had been jumped on by monkeys.

Everywhere lurked the memory of Fletcher. Throughout the cutting of Gerry's movie, she had had no time to sit down and think about him, though she knew eventually she must. Hard experience had proved to her that troubles could not be exiled from the heart, only stuffed into dark corners where they tended to ferment and stew. Left too long, they might explode like Fletcher's pressure cooker. If she was ever to have peace again, she would have to *make* that peace with her multilayered memories.

Unpacked but far from settled in, Carla took a long, roaming walk through Manhattan, reacquainting herself with her city. No matter how crazy it made her, or how heavy the pressure it put on her heart, she loved this island. Southern California had been a drug, lulling her into lethargy until the editing job had come along. The hell-bent pace of *this* aggressive city suited her better. It kept up with the pulse of her own blood. She thrived on urgency and high energy—as she had thrived on the atmosphere Fletcher cast about him. She wouldn't deny that. Those short, frenetic days in his company had invigorated her beyond measure.

She caught herself walking down Fifty-seventh Street, unconsciously scanning the lunchtime crowds for sight of him. Castigating herself, she hurried on to Seventh Avenue, only to drift up to and around Central Park in a blue mood. He had been good for her, she could admit that now. She had always thought she was *protecting* the tender Carla; he had made her see that she was smothering her. The inner Carla was not only tender. She was strong and demanding, passionate, inspired and frightening in her intensity. To keep that passion under control Carla had needed to distort everything to an explanation that fit. She had been hurt, yes, to find that Fletcher had pretended ignorance through even their most intimate moments, and she had reacted with unreasoning anger. But that hadn't really been it—the truth was that she had been afraid to face the emotions he called up from her. She had been all too willing to plaster the handiest explanation over the chaos of her feelings, like wallpaper over a crumbling wall, and walk away, hoping it would hold.

He *hadn't* used her to advance Mercy's career. Never once had he even mentioned anything as crass as Bob Rhoades's favor theory. His only crime had been to know what she hadn't wanted known and, as Valerie had pointed out in sincere apology for herself and Gerry, he couldn't *help* knowing, and he had *tried*.

After this admission came the hardest one Carla had yet to make—it was entirely possible that Fletcher had loved her. As she realized where her unruly feet had taken her— to the flagstone sidewalk in front of his fortresslike apartment building—she choked back a melancholy noise. This coming to terms business was just as hard as she had feared; as surely as she knew she had destroyed Fletcher's love for her, she knew her own love for him had survived.

Annette lounged with her feet on Fletcher's desk and a film trade paper in her lap.

"My, you have made yourself at home since you became the manager of a movie star," Fletcher observed tolerantly. He had just come in from the dank, chill December afternoon and his cheeks held what resembled a healthy glow, so different from the pallor that had afflicted him all fall. He knew Annette would approve of this; she had taken to mothering him. He put it down to her increased sense of responsibility and self-confidence as a partner in the company.

"Don't let Mercy hear you say that," his partner warned. "She's not a star *yet*." Then she grinned. "But soon! How was that band in New Jersey?"

Fletcher looked sour. "With a new lead singer and about three more years of practice they could work up to bad."

"Oh...you'll find someone, Fletch."

He plopped down on the couch, closing his eyes and sinking into a rare pose of rest. "I know. There's no hurry. But sometimes I wonder whether the bands are really as dull as I think them or if I've just lost whatever it takes to get excited...."

"Maybe you could use a vacation?"

"What? You mean fall into a coma around some pool in Montserrat, surrounded by bathing beauties? You know I'd lose my marbles from boredom."

"Yeah, I suppose so. It's not a problem other people have though."

They fell into a companionable silence. Annette perused her paper devotedly, as caught up in the excitement of films as Fletcher had once been in that of music. Fletcher let himself drift off....

"Well!"

Annette's low exclamation roused him. "What?"

She pursed her lips. "Oh, it's probably not something that would interest you."

"Do I look like I've got something *else* on my mind?"

"No, but...well, you'd probably find it annoying...."

"I'm finding *this* annoying!" he exclaimed in mock aggravation. "Just *tell* me already."

Annette's eyes flickered, then she read, "'Opening tonight, at the Fifty-fourth Street Showplace is the new Gerry Martin/John Kramer film *The Pacesetter*, which was rumored to be in terminal difficulties due to the inexperience of its young director. Preliminary screenings have resulted in the new rumor that it has been snatched from the abyss by the brilliant surgery of Martin's film editors—wife Valerie Martin and a young, east coast independent video producer, Carla Abbott-Copeland. And if that name rings any bells in your mind, it should—Carla's mom is none other than the Earhart of cinema, producer Amelia Abbott-Copeland.'"

Fletcher's slanted eyes slid away from contact with Annette's. "Hmmm..."

Annette picked up the comment and continued blandly. "Wonder what made her change her mind. I thought she intended to die an old documentary maker in the heart of Hell's Kitchen. Guess that should be a lesson to all of us— even the most obstinate fanatic can be made to see sense."

"Don't get carried away," Fletcher growled.

"Maybe you're right. Well, too bad she didn't have a change of heart while she was working here. You'd be a teen idol now, just like Billy."

"*Please*!"

She laughed and set her feet on the floor. "Well, I'm off. What are your plans for the evening?"

"Another club...on the West Side somewhere."

"Good luck." She swatted him on the knee and left.

Fletcher remained unmoved, eyes closed, in his darkening office, but his mind churned. Carla Abbott-Copeland. . .Carla Abbott-Copeland on a Gerry Martin film, no less! Why *hadn't* she come around earlier? Why hadn't she come around during one of the many times he had had her in his arms, when he could have held on to her and made her believe, before everything had come crashing in on their heads? His dejection at losing her in that way had never left him. It colored every moment of his life a bleak gray; it leeched his energy, his excitement, his optimism. Even MAY, the pet project that had absorbed so much of his altruistic devotion, failed to satisfy him anymore. Only force of habit made him swing by the clubs hoping to feel the old spark. He didn't even have the energy to resent her; he felt flattened into careless apathy. At least it wouldn't happen to him again.

Who was he kidding? It could happen again—she could make it happen again. One look from those huge, haunted eyes and his heart would quicken, even if it was only to break once again.

All afternoon before the premiere Carla's stomach fluttered and her head threatened to ache. December had refused to get cold enough to turn the endless, dreary rain to snow and the streets teamed with soggy, overbundled Christmas shoppers in various states of bad humor. The only optimistic thought that struck Carla all day was that the sporadic rain might thin the crowds expected outside the theater that night.

She dreaded the evening, but at the appointed hour she forced herself into a raspberry silk dress that wouldn't shame her if she had the bad luck to get in the way of a TV camera. She pinned her hair up in a knot, watching in resignation as tendrils sprang out, and put her feet into new pumps that would never survive a drop of rain.

Three blocks before the theater the traffic started to snarl. Carla hadn't seen so many stretch limousines in her entire life. Fans and reporters ran in and out between cars, peering through the tinted windshields, trying to determine who rode inside. Thank God she looked like an ordinary nobody on her way to a normal party, Carla thought.

"Lady, I don't think I can get you any farther," the cabbie announced around the damp stump of his cigar. They had sat at the corner of Fifty-fourth and Seventh Avenue for over five minutes, unable to make the turn. Carla felt sick to her stomach from the tension and the smoke.

"Thanks anyway, I guess I'll hoof it from here." She got out money to pay him.

"If you're trying to get anywhere near the place where they're showing that new movie you'd better skip it—they got security like you wouldn't believe."

He thought her another sightseer. She smiled grimly and fingered the gilt-edged invitation in her evening bag. "Unfortunately, I'm supposed to be there."

She could see his frown in the rearview mirror. "Are you somebody famous? If you don't mind my asking."

"No, sorry. I'm just one of the film editors."

Before he could admit to not knowing what a film editor did, she escaped onto the sidewalk. At least the rain had not started. Down the block the white beams of powerful spotlights swept the night, revealing the overcast sky. A huge marquee had been lit with the names of the film and its stars, and platforms ringed the entrance to hold camera crews from the television networks. Press and amateur photographers dove ambitiously through the milling crowds. Limo after limo slipped up to the theater and deposited its load of celebrities.

The closer Carla got, the slower her legs would work. A sullen dread had taken over her chest and stomach. How in the world would she make herself push up to the barricades and flash her invitation? The whole procedure appalled her. She realized she had frozen in her tracks, unable to go another step. What did all this pomp have to do with her work? She might have gone back to the Hollywood world, but that didn't mean it had turned her into an exhibitionist. Stuffing the invitation deep into her coat pocket, she turned away and set off back down the block. With great luck, she might make it home dry.

The film would be a success without her; she needn't feel she had failed the Martins by chickening out on the premiere. Premieres were showcases for the stars, anyway, not the stagehands. So wrapped up in this reasoning was Carla that she failed to notice the figure that materialized from the crowd and stuck by her. With a start she looked up—it was Fletcher. Her heart beat so hard she thought it would break through her ribs. Wrapped in a long sweeping black coat, he looked as magnificent as her memories had insisted, if perhaps a little pale.

"You decided not to go to the premiere," he observed.

"Oh...yes...How did you know about it?"

He shrugged evasively. "Annette's always telling me what's going on in the world, even if it has nothing to do with rock."

"Ah," she replied inadequately. Why was he walking with her? "I didn't see you in the crowd by the theater."

"No, I was sitting in a restaurant across the street killing time until this club opens that I'm going to check out tonight."

"A new client?"

"Hopefully." He seemed able to talk a little more easily on this neutral subject. "They've already got a manager, but the grapevine says they don't think he's doing enough for them. I thought I'd go see if they were worth stealing.''

"I hear Mercy and Billy are doing well."

"Yes, we've been lucky. Billy's album went platinum a week ago, in fact. And Mercy got the movie role she had her heart set on. Annette's doing a good job with her."

"Good..." Carla remarked inadequately. His appearance had put her so off balance she felt she had the brain power of a pigeon.

"How about you? Working on another big film?"

"Oh, no. Since I got back to the city in October I've been doing a little video of my own."

"Another documentary?"

She checked his face for any sign of irony and found nothing but sincere interest. "No, actually, it's an idea I came up with while cutting *The Pacesetter*. Sort of an art film on the kids who exercise racehorses and muck out the stalls and stuff for no money, hoping to be jockeys or trainers or whatever. They're really special kids—totally obsessed with horses. From Gerry's film I got to wonder about what keeps them going through such hard work. It'll never make a dime, I suppose, not like the documentaries."

He nodded. She decided that his diplomacy was part of what unnerved her. "Aren't you going to say 'I told you so'?"

He looked surprised. "What did I tell you?"

"That I wasn't a journalist, remember? That I'd never be satisfied with documentaries."

"Well, you can never tell anybody anything they don't already know deep down inside."

"Don't be so modest. It was damn *deep* all right."

As he continued to walk along with his serious eyes fixed on his toes, she felt moved to say, "I guess I have you to thank for jolting me awake. I didn't do a very good job of thanking you before, did I?''

He shook off her apology. ''I had no right to provoke you so much.... I'm not usually such a barbarian.''

They were silent for a few steps, Carla because the sadness had welled in her, realizing that, had he loved her once, he might have indeed thought it his right to provoke her. Trying again for lightness, she remarked, ''Hey, you're used to dealing with temperamental artists—most of them are, I guess.''

He smiled softly. ''So you turned out to be coolheaded after all, huh, Fellini?''

The use of the nickname made her catch her breath. Covering up for it, she plunged into a blithe explanation. ''Oh, not at all. I'm all emotionally wrapped up in this new video—no more objective journalism. It's my feelings and point of view all the way with this one. I just don't throw temper tantrums anymore. I mean, I *might* someday, but it'd have to be a drastic situation.''

''I see.''

Carla frowned. She felt as if she was missing something critical, some key to his careful cordiality. Beyond that, why did she continue to walk with him? She had passed her turn-off onto Tenth Avenue half a block back. Just as she was about to give up and bid him good night, Fletcher inquired blandly, ''So how is it up there on Mount Olympus?''

So now the rancor started to show. She had been afraid that his forgiveness only went so far. . .Yet it irked her because it reminded her of yet another habit she would have to break—that of expecting Fletcher's boundless generosity. ''I *did* say I was sorry, Fletcher,'' she pointed out quietly. ''I *meant* it, more than the words get across. And I *did* destroy that video.''

"Yes, at the last possible moment you saved my reputation." His sarcasm surprised her, and it went oddly with the bright smile that flashed in the corners of his mouth.

Nettled, she asked, "If you weren't satisfied, why didn't you come talk to me a long time ago?"

"Why, I was scared to death."

"Of *me*?"

He grinned broadly, swung around a corner to the awning-covered entrance of a Twelfth Avenue rock club. "Ah, here we are. Coming in with me?"

"Of course I am! I can't let you escape with this idiotic notion that I'm an unreasonable, stuck-up prig!" A further reason fell from the sky in drenching cold splats—the rain had started. Carla trotted willingly up the steps of the club with Fletcher. She reached the door first and found that a burly arm blocked her way.

"Sorry, closed house tonight, honey," the door guard growled.

In irritation, Carla looked toward Fletcher. He sauntered up to the guard, hands stuffed negligently in his coat pockets and an inexplicable look of good humor on his handsome face.

"Who's the band tonight? The Savages?"

"That's right."

"That's who I came to see all right."

"Sorry. It's sort of a private party."

"You mean you have an exclusive guest list."

"That's right," the guard agreed monotonously.

What was the delay? Carla wondered. Surely Fletcher had arranged to get on their stupid guest list.... He leaned complacently against the railing, showing no special hurry. "I never thought the Savages had a reputation for exclusive door policies."

The guard shrugged.

"In fact, I never thought the Savages had any kind of reputation at *all*."

"Just doing my job, man," came the grumpy reply.

Fletcher nodded understandingly and backed down a step. "Guess that's it, Carla."

He had to be kidding! The rain was coming down in buckets, they were two feet away from the inside of a warm, dry club and he wasn't going to go in? He didn't even wait to see if she would follow, just retreated back to the sidewalk, turning up his collar. Incredulous, she stormed after him. "Fletcher!"

He waited for her then.

"Fletcher! Tell him you're expected!"

"But I'm not."

"That's a minor detail. He works at a *rock* club, he'll recognize your name...hell, tell him you're going to manage this band!"

"I'm not sure I want to. It takes an awful lot of gall to get snotty about who you let in to see you when you don't even have any following yet. I'm not sure I could work with this band."

"You're just a reverse snob! It used to be nothing to you to breeze through this kind of celebrity garbage."

His eyes snapped at her in indignation. "And it used to be *death* to you. Now you want me to pull rank because Carla *Abbott-Copeland* is a little wet, don't you?"

She planted her feet, in their squishy ruined shoes, firmly apart and yelled in the deserted street. "Number one—I did not sell out, chuck my ethics, or whatever you think, just because I decided to be myself, Fletcher Arendt! And number two—I'm not 'a little wet', I'm *drowning*! And if *you're* planning on swimming up to that cushy penthouse of yours, you can just do it *alone*! I'm going back to that stupid club and drop as many names as I have to until they let me in to phone a taxi!'' Unable to make sense of his delighted expression, she spun away to make good her pronouncement. His hand snagged her in midturn and both arms settled around her waist, preventing any more escapes. Even through their heavy coats, she could feel the warm strength of his achingly familiar body. The rain running over his high cheeks, bejeweling his lashes, brought stabbing home the memory of the last time rain had caught the two of them...rain and passion, she remembered, rain and love.

"A drastic situation, huh?'' he suggested sweetly.

"You think you're pretty clever, don't you?'' she retaliated, making no move to get away. "Getting me all riled up after I've been bragging about how reasonable I've become.''

"That wasn't cleverness, that was instinct. I was *clever* in being able to find you again.''

She couldn't help spreading her fingers against the fabric of the coat that so cruelly separated her from the beautiful swell of his golden chest—was it pale now, too? In a low, uncertain voice, eyes raised no higher than his collar, she asked, "What did you want to find me for?''

He answered her with a kiss, a sweet, tender, provoking explanation that served better than words. Her arms rose and twined ardently around his neck and her body melted like sugar into his embrace. All crazy thought drained from her mind in the presence of blissful relief. How had life suddenly become so right? She had done nothing to deserve it, nothing to merit the love of this splendid man. When his mouth finally separated from hers, she whispered wonderingly, "But aren't you mad at me for the way I've been acting?''

Intoxicating as wine, his rich voice soaked through her. "I hope I'm not *such* an ogre. You've been making a lot of hard adjustments lately. I may tease, but I know it's not easy to carry that big name around. You're bound to be a little prickly until you get used to it.''

''If I *ever* do.''

He gazed down on her speculatively, a soft light in his cloudless blue eyes. ''I have an idea that could make it easier.''

''What?''

''You could drop the 'Abbott-Copeland' business, change your name to something that has no weight in the movie world at all.''

''And what name is that?''

''Arendt.''

''Boy, no one would give me the time of day if I were named Carla Arendt. I like it.''

''Good. But it's the last one you get, you know. You're just going to have to live with Carla *Arendt*.''

''As long as you'll be living with her, too.''

''Not in that loft, though—I'm holding out for the cushy penthouse.''

''What's wrong with my loft?'' she protested. ''It's warmer than this street corner.''

Concern darkened his face and he stroked a finger over her lips. ''You're shaking! I *have* let you get too cold.''

''Yes, you have. What do you propose to do about it?''

He bent to her ear to whisper his answer.

READERS' COMMENTS ON SILHOUETTE ROMANCES:

If you're ready for a more sensual, more provocative reading experience...

We'll send you **4** Silhouette Desire novels **FREE...**

and without obligation

Then, we'll send you six more Silhouette Desire® novels to preview every month for 15 days with absolutely no obligation!

When you decide to keep them, you pay just $1.95 each ($2.25, in Canada), *with no shipping, handling, or additional charges of any kind!*

Silhouette Desire novels are not for everyone. They are written especially for the woman who wants a more satisfying, more deeply involving reading experience.

Silhouette Desire novels take you *beyond* the others and offer real-life drama and romance of successful women in charge of their lives. You'll share precious, private moments and secret dreams... experience every whispered word of love, every ardent touch, every passionate heartbeat.

As a home subscriber, you will also receive FREE, a subscription to the Silhouette Books Newsletter as long as you remain a member. Each issue is filled with news on upcoming titles, interviews with your favorite authors, even their favorite recipes.

And, the first 4 Silhouette Books are absolutely FREE and without obligation, yours to keep! What could be easier... and where else could you find such a satisfying reading experience?

To get your free books, fill out and return the coupon today!

Silhouette ❤ Desire®

Silhouette Books, 120 Brighton Rd., P.O. Box 5084, Clifton, NJ 07015-5084

COMING NEXT MONTH

WRITTEN ON THE WIND—Rita Rainville
Handwriting expert Dena Trevor went undercover to discover a
security leak at Brand McAllister's company, and in the process she
discovered love.

GILDING THE LILY—Emilie Richards
Lesley Belmont had never thought of herself as a beautiful or
desirable woman, but to cartoonist Travis Hagers she was
devastating.

KINDRED HEARTS—Lacey Springer
Laine Morgan had responsibilities to her family and a career she
loved. Would she be forced to choose between her life-style and the
man she loved?

EYE OF THE BEHOLDER—Charlotte Nichols
Daina Wellsfry was generally a very good judge of character, but
when she met Clay Wilde she realized that she had a lot to learn
about people…and herself.

NOW OR NEVER—Arlene James
Taking in boarders had been merely a way for Mary to make extra
money, until Nolan Tanner rented the room, and she realized that
her life would never be the same.

CHRISTMAS MASQUERADE—Debbie Macomber
Jo Marie had finally met her dream man. Andrew fulfilled her every
fantasy, until she discovered that he was engaged to another
woman, and that woman was her best friend.

AVAILABLE NOW:

Please Stand By
Marie Nicole

Forgotten Love
Phyllis Halldorson

The Matthews Affair
Victoria Glenn

With Marriage In Mind
Dorothy Cork

The Sea at Dawn
Laurie Paige

Camera Shy
Lynnette Morland